Alternative Medicine

Other Books of Related Interest:

Opposing Viewpoints Series

Eating Disorders

Health Care

At Issue Series

Alcohol Abuse

Food Insecurity

Health Care Legislation

Current Controversies Series

Medicare

Pollution

Vaccines

"Congress shall make
no law ... abridging
the freedom of speech,
or of the press."

First Amendment to the US Constitution

The basic foundation of our democracy is the First Amendment guarantee of freedom of expression. The Opposing Viewpoints series is dedicated to the concept of this basic freedom and the idea that it is more important to practice it than to enshrine it.

OPPOSING
VIEWPOINTS®
SERIES

Alternative Medicine

Lynn M. Zott, Book Editor

GREENHAVEN PRESS
A part of Gale, Cengage Learning

GALE
CENGAGE Learning·

Detroit • New York • San Francisco • New Haven, Conn • Waterville, Maine • London

Elizabeth Des Chenes, *Director, Publishing Solutions*

© 2012 Greenhaven Press, a part of Gale, Cengage Learning.

Gale and Greenhaven Press are registered trademarks used herein under license.

For more information, contact:
Greenhaven Press
27500 Drake Rd.
Farmington Hills, MI 48331-3535
Or you can visit our Internet site at gale.cengage.com

For product information and technology assistance, contact us at

Gale Customer Support, 1-800-877-4253
For permission to use material from this text or product, submit all requests online at
www.cengage.com/permissions

Further permissions questions can be emailed to permissionrequest@cengage.com

Articles in Greenhaven Press anthologies are often edited for length to meet page requirements. In addition, original titles of these works are changed to clearly present the main thesis and to explicitly indicate the author's opinion. Every effort is made to ensure that Greenhaven Press accurately reflects the original intent of the authors. Every effort has been made to trace the owners of copyrighted material.

Cover Image copyright © Piotr Rzeszutek/Shuttershock.com.

LIBRARY OF CONGRESS CATALOGING-IN-PUBLICATION DATA

Alternative medicine / Lynn M. Zott, book editor.
  p. cm. -- (Opposing viewpoints)
Summary: "Alternative Medicine: Opposing Viewpoints is the leading source for libraries and classrooms in need of current-issue materials. The viewpoints are selected from a wide range of highly respected sources and publications"--Provided by publisher.
  Includes bibliographical references and index.
  ISBN 978-0-7377-5438-4 (hardback)--ISBN 978-0-7377-5439-1 (paperback)
  1. Alternative medicine--Juvenile literature. I. Zott, Lynn M. (Lynn Marie), 1969-
R733.A4587 2012
610--dc23
                                                              2012005371

Printed in Mexico
2 3 4 5 6 7 16 15 14 13 12

Contents

Why Consider Opposing Viewpoints?   **11**

Introduction   **14**

Chapter 1: Does Alternative Medicine Work?

Chapter Preface   **20**

1. Homeopathic Medicine Is Effective   **23**
   Dana Ullman

2. Homeopathic Medicine Is Ineffective   **35**
   Edzard Ernst

3. Sham Acupuncture's Effectiveness Casts Doubt on the Efficacy of Real Acupuncture   **40**
   Ted Burnham

4. Acupuncture Is Effective Despite Research Showing That Sham Acupuncture Is Helpful   **47**
   John Amaro

5. Chelation Therapy Is a Safe and Effective Treatment for Many Conditions   **53**
   Elmer M. Cranton

6. Chelation Therapy Is Dangerous and Ineffective for Treating Most Health Problems   **65**
   Saul Green

Periodical and Internet Sources Bibliography   **77**

Chapter 2: Why Is Alternative Medicine Popular?

Chapter Preface   **79**

1. Politics and Culture Contribute to Alternative Medicine's Popularity   **82**
   Rahul Parikh

2. The Popularity of Alternative Medicine   **90**
   Is Exaggerated
   Brennen McKenzie

3. The Prevalence of Complementary Treatments   **98**
   Reflects Frustration with Traditional Medicine
   Lauren Cox

4. Celebrities Influence Public Interest in   **105**
   Alternative Treatments That Can Be Detrimental
   Liz Szabo

Periodical and Internet Sources Bibliography   **112**

Chapter 3: Can Alternative and Conventional Medicine Work Together?

Chapter Preface   **114**

1. The Need for Improvements in Health Care   **117**
   Highlights the Advantages of Integrative
   Medicine
   Donald Berwick (and Andrea M. Schultz,
   Samantha M. Chao, J. Michael McGinnis)

2. A Complementary Medical Treatment Approach   **126**
   Can Lower Health Care Costs
   Kathleen Koster

3. A Complementary Approach to Medicine Helps   **134**
   Patients and Is Scientifically Sound
   David Katz

4. Complementary Medicine Is Scientifically   **144**
   Unsound and Only Increases Provider Profits
   Ben Kavoussi

5. Doctors Can and Should Regularly Use Ethically   **153**
   Prescribed Placebo Treatments
   Steve Silberman

6. Placebo Treatment Can Have Harmful   167
   as Well as Beneficial Effects
   Eliezer Sobel

Periodical and Internet Sources Bibliography   174

Chapter 4: How Should Government Research and Regulate Alternative Medicine?

Chapter Preface   176

1. The National Center for Complementary and   179
   Alternative Medicine Should Be Funded
   *National Center for Complementary
   and Alternative Medicine*

2. The National Center for Complementary and   191
   Alternative Medicine Should Not Be Funded
   David Gorski

3. The Value of the National Center   204
   for Complementary and Alternative Medicine
   Is Unclear
   David Brown

4. Expanding Labeling Requirements Would Better   211
   Inform Consumers About Safe Supplement Use
   The Office of Senator Dick Durbin

5. Expanding Labeling Requirements   216
   for Dietary Supplements Would Punish
   Consumers and Manufacturers
   Hank Schultz and Todd Runestad

Periodical and Internet Sources Bibliography   224

For Further Discussion   225

Organizations to Contact   230

Bibliography of Books   238

Index   242

want to be violated in that way,'" Isaacson recalls in an interview on the television program *60 Minutes*, which aired on October 23, 2011. "So he waited nine months, while his wife and others urged him to do it, before getting the operation," added Isaacson.

"Mr. Jobs allegedly chose to undergo all sorts of alternative treatment options before opting for conventional medicine," commented Ramzi Amri, a cancer research associate and Fulbright scholar at Harvard Medical School, in an October 12, 2011, post on the website Quora. Amri continued, asserting: "This was, of course, a freedom he had all the rights to take, but given the circumstances it seems sound to assume that Mr. Jobs' choice for alternative medicine could have led to an unnecessarily early death." Because Jobs's neuroendocrine tumor was a relatively rare, typically slow-growing variety that has a high-cure rate following full surgical removal, Amri maintained, Jobs's chances for a full recovery would have been very high if he had not delayed the proper treatment. Some commentators have taken issue with Amri's claims, saying there is no way to be certain what Jobs's chances of recovery were because the precise type of tumor he had was never confirmed by clinical testing. Others however have endorsed Amri's view and have echoed Ryan Tate's assertion in an October 20, 2011, post on Gawker.com that "Jobs's instinct for defiant iconoclasm and his insistence on unconventional approaches did not, in the end, serve him as well as it served Apple's customers and shareholders. And it seems clear Jobs knew this, and wanted the rest of us to know it, too."

Indeed, even proponents of alternative medicine or integrative medicine—the term used to describe a collaborative approach that combines conventional and alternative medicine—maintain that conventional medicine is crucial in treating traumatic injury and aggressive illnesses such as cancer. Perhaps the most famous champion of integrative medicine, Dr. Andrew Weil, as quoted on his website, DrWeil.com, said,

"If I were hit by a bus, I'd want to be taken immediately to a high-tech emergency room." While alternative medicine practices such as yoga, acupuncture, meditation, and herbal medicine, including the use of medical marijuana to treat the nausea associated with chemotherapy, are recommended to cancer patients by their oncologists, they are meant as *supplements* to conventional treatments for cancer such as surgery, radiation, and chemotherapy, rather than as an *alternative* to such treatments. Doctors and other public health advocates frequently condemn what they view as the ethically abhorrent and medically dangerous practice of offering unproven alternative "cures" to vulnerable cancer patients, many of whom have been diagnosed as having terminal disease by conventional doctors. Furthermore, the American Cancer Society's website warns patients to avoid alternative treatments that "promise a cure for all cancers"; advise patients to avoid "recommended or standard medical treatment"; "claim to offer benefits, but no side effects"; require patients to "travel to another country"; "use terms like 'scientific breakthrough,' 'miracle cure,' 'secret ingredient,' or 'ancient remedy'"; offer "personal stories of amazing results, but no actual scientific evidence"; or whose "promoters attack the medical or scientific community." And yet a June 8, 2009, *USA Today* article by Marilynn Marchione reports that 60 percent of cancer patients try alternative medicine therapies.

Reports of cases like that of Ruth Phillips, who was cured of mesothelioma—a form of cancer caused by exposure to asbestos whose victims usually die within two years of diagnosis—after receiving immuno augmentative therapy (IAT), a controversial alternative approach to treatment offered by a clinic in the Bahamas, continue to defy research study results and spark debate over the efficacy of alternative treatments. According to a September 28, 2011, article posted on the website Asbestos.com, which is sponsored by the Mesothelioma Center, "Ruth Phillips took her eight-months-to-live mesothelioma diagnosis from one highly regarded cancer center to another—from Atlanta to New York to Washington, D.C.—and it hardly changed. Doctors painted a picture she refused to accept. So she gambled. And won. Phillips flew to Freeport, Bahamas, not for the sun and the fun and not to spend her final days at some glitzy casino resort. She rolled the dice in a different game, stepping into a controversial, outside-the-box, alternative treatment clinic that looked nothing like the fancy cancer centers she had been visiting. That was 12 years ago. Today Phillips is thriving, returning home from another workout at a local gymnasium, preparing to make dinner for her husband, not worried about the mesothelioma that should have killed her long ago."

"We seem to be able to control the growth of tumors. Rather, we can get a person's immune system to control them," John Clement, the director of the Bahamian IAT clinic told Asbestos.com. "It doesn't work all the time, but our results exceed anyone else's." The US Food and Drug Administration (FDA) has banned the use of IAT in the United States, although according to the Asbestos.com article there are now some American cancer research centers that are investigating and using variations of IAT to treat various types of cancer. The American Cancer Society, in a Cancer.org post discussing IAT, declares: "Available scientific evidence does not support claims that IAT is effective in treating people with cancer. Success stories associated with the treatment are based mainly on individual reports ..., and they include little or no supporting evidence."

The controversy over nontraditional cancer treatments is just one aspect of the debate over complementary and alternative medicine explored in *Opposing Viewpoints: Alternative Medicine*. The viewpoints in this book explore the medical, social, legal, and ethical concerns surrounding the use of alternative medicine in the following chapters: Does Alternative Medicine Work?, Why Is Alternative Medicine Popular?, Can

Alternative and Conventional Medicine Work Together?, and How Should Government Research and Regulate Alternative Medicine? The information provided in this volume provides insight into some of the recent controversies surrounding issues such as the results and evidence provided by clinical trials and other studies of alternative therapies; the efficacy of alternative remedies such as homeopathy, chelation therapy, and acupuncture; the role of the placebo effect in alternative and conventional medicine; the use of public funding for the purpose of studying alternative therapies; and the legislation of dietary supplement manufacturing and labeling.

OPPOSING
VIEWPOINTS®
SERIES

CHAPTER 1

Does Alternative Medicine Work?

Chapter Preface

Of the alternative medical approaches that have been subjected to the rigors of clinical trials, the one that has yielded the most consistent positive results is the practice of meditation. Acceptance of the wide variety of health benefits offered by regular meditation is widespread among mainstream doctors and researchers, and clinical evidence has been viewed as potentially revolutionary in the study of how certain lifestyle changes can impact overall health and well-being. In a January 28, 2011, *New York Times* article, Sindya N. Bhanoo reported on a study in which "researchers report that those who meditated for about 30 minutes a day for eight weeks had measurable changes in gray-matter density in parts of the brain associated with memory, sense of self, empathy and stress."[1] Bhanoo added that "MRI brain scans taken before and after the participants' meditation regimen found increased gray matter in the hippocampus, an area important for learning and memory. The images also showed a reduction of gray matter in the amygdala, a region connected to anxiety and stress. A control group that did not practice meditation showed no such changes." Other studies have also documented and confirmed that there are significant differences between the brains of regular practitioners of meditation and non-practitioners. Furthermore, neuroscientists have shown great interest in studying the effects of meditation as part of exploring neuroplasticity, which is the capacity of the brain to change and develop new neural networks, or connections between areas of the brain, as a result of the experience.

Holistic nursing practitioner R. Bonadonna has asserted that "clinical effects of meditation impact a broad spectrum of physical and psychological symptoms and syndromes, including reduced anxiety, pain, and depression, enhanced mood and self-esteem, and decreased stress. . . . Meditation practice can positively influence the experience of chronic illness and can serve as a primary, secondary, and/or tertiary prevention strategy.... Living mindfully with chronic illness is a fruitful area for research, and it can be predicted that evidence will grow to support the role of consciousness in the human experience of disease."[2] A study published in 2009, in which African American men and women diagnosed with coronary artery disease—a narrowing of the blood vessels to the heart that is a major factor in death from heart attack or stroke, especially among African Americans—participated in a Transcendental Meditation program, concluded: "Stress reduction with the Transcendental Meditation program was associated with 43% reduction in risk for all cause[s of] mortality, myocardial infarction [heart attack] and stroke."[3] A study published in 2003 indicated that there is a possibility that meditation also has immune-boosting potential, concluding: "These findings demonstrate that a short program in mindfulness meditation produces demonstrable effects on brain and immune function. These findings suggest that meditation may change brain and immune function in positive ways and underscore the need for additional research."[4]

The effectiveness of various types of alternative therapies and their implications for public health are examined in detail in this chapter of *Opposing Viewpoints: Alternative Medicine*. The viewpoints in this chapter explore the debate over the relative benefits and dangers associated with popular alternative treatment methods, focusing especially on homeopathy, acupuncture, and chelation therapy.

Notes

1. Sindya N. Bhanoo, "How Meditation May Change the Brain," *New York Times*, January 28, 2011. http://well.blogs .nytimes.com.

2. R. Bonadonna, "Meditation's Impact on Chronic Illness," *Holistic Nursing Practice*, vol. 17, no. 6, November–December 2003, p. 309.

3. Robert Schneider et al., "Abstract 1177: Effects of Stress Reduction on Clinical Events in African Americans with Coronary Heart Disease: A Randomized Controlled Trial," *Circulation*, vol. 120, 2009, p. S461.

4. Richard J. Davidson et al., "Alterations in Brain and Immune Function Produced by Mindfulness Meditation," *Psychosomatic Medicine*, vol. 65, no. 4, July–August 2003, p. 564.

"It is the ideological and financial threat that homeopathy poses that motivates the antagonism to it, not whether it works or not."

Homeopathic Medicine Is Effective

Dana Ullman

Dana Ullman is a practitioner and advocate of homeopathy, a columnist for the Huffington Post, *the founder of Homeopathic Educational Services, and the author of several books including* The Homeopathic Revolution: Why Famous People and Cultural Heroes Choose Homeopathy. *In the following viewpoint, Ullman challenges the claims of critics of homeopathy that scientific research has proven that it is ineffective. He argues that most scientific research is itself highly flawed, as are conclusions drawn from it. Ullman maintains that conventional medicine's reliance upon medications that alleviate symptoms of disease is not only based on faulty science, but also is harmful because it hampers the human body's natural defense against disease. Ullman also decries what he views as a profit-driven manipulation of scientific data to benefit drug manufacturers and other companies in the health care industry. Homeopathy and other forms of naturopathic medicine, Ullman explains, work with and enhance the body's natural defenses to assist it in healing itself. He addresses many criticisms of homeopathy, citing the research and analyses that have shown that homeopathy is effective, and he predicts that the medical community will soon accept and embrace the homeopathic model of healing.*

As you read, consider the following questions:

1. What does Ullman say that research has shown to be true about the effectiveness of antidepressants vs. placebos?

2. What, according to Ullman, were the profits earned by the ten largest drug companies in 2002?

3. How does Ullman describe homeopaths' definition and use of the concept of "vital force"?

Mahatma Gandhi was once asked by a reporter what he thought about Western civilization, and in light of the uncivilized treatment by the British government of his nonviolent actions, he immediately replied, "Western civilization? Yes, it is a good idea." Likewise, if he were asked what he thought about "scientific medicine," he would probably have replied in a similar manner.

The idea of scientific medicine is a great one, but is modern medicine truly, or even adequately, "scientific"?

Modern medicine uses the double-blind and placebo-controlled trial as the gold standard by which the effectiveness of a treatment is determined. On the surface, this scientific method is very reasonable. However, serious problems in these studies are widely acknowledged by academics but remain unknown to the general public. *Fundamental questions about the meaning of the word "efficacy" are rarely raised.*

For instance, just because a drug treatment seems to eliminate a specific symptom does not necessarily mean that it is "effective." In fact, getting rid of a specific symptom can be the bad news. Aspirin may lower your fever, but physiologists recognize that fever is an important defense of the body in its efforts to fight infection. Sleep-inducing drugs may lead you to fall asleep, but they do not lead to refreshed sleep, and these drugs ultimately tend to aggravate the cycle of insomnia and fatigue, while conveniently (for the drug companies) tend to create addiction. Long-term safety and efficacy of many modern drugs for common ailments remain unknown, despite the high hopes and sincere expectations from the medical community and the rest of us for greater certainty.

Scientific Research Is Easily and Often Manipulated

The bottom line to scientific research is that a scientist can set up a study that shows the guise of efficacy. In other words, a drug may be effective for a very limited period of time and then cause various serious symptoms. For example, a very popular antianxiety drug called Xanax was shown to reduce panic attacks during a two-month experiment, but when individuals reduce or stop the medication, panic attacks can increase 300–400 percent. Would many patients take this drug if they knew this fact, and based on what standard can anyone honestly say that this drug is "effective"?

To get FDA approval to market a drug, most of the studies for psychiatric conditions last only six weeks. In view of the fact that most people take antidepressant or antianxiety medicines for years, can these short studies be scientifically valid? What is so little known and so sobering is that research to date has found that placebos are 80 percent as effective and have fewer side effects and [are] a lot cheaper.

Marcia Angell, MD, the former editor of the *New England Journal of Medicine* and author of the powerful book *The Truth About the Drug Companies*, said it plainly and directly: "Trials can be rigged in a dozen ways, and it happens all the time."

She further expresses real concern about research reliability:

> It is simply no longer possible to believe much of the clinical research that is published, or to rely on the judgment of trusted physicians or authoritative medical guidelines. I take no pleasure in this conclusion, which I reached slowly and reluctantly over my two decades as an editor of the *New England Journal of Medicine*. As reprehensible as many industry practices are, I believe the behavior of much of the medical profession is even more culpable.

Angell gives many examples of why reading research studies is not reliable:

> A review of 74 clinical trials of antidepressants, for example, found that 37 of 38 positive studies were published. *But of the thirty-six negative studies, thirty-three were either not published or published in a form that conveyed a positive outcome.*

Conventional drugs used today are so new that there is very little long-term research on them. There are good reasons why a vast majority of modern drugs used just a couple of decades ago are no longer prescribed: They don't work as well as previously assumed, and/or they cause more harm than good.

Reliance on Drugs Reflects a Flawed Approach to Healing

Sadly and strangely, many physicians do not see that there is something fundamentally wrong with the present medical model. Once a drug is found to be ineffective or dangerous, doctors and drug companies simply find another drug that, at least initially, seems to have good short-term results, that is, until longer term studies establish that it doesn't work as well as assumed and/or is more dangerous. Although some people consider these failures as evidence of the wisdom of the scientific process, these problems are evidence of the limitations of a model of medicine that overemphasizes a biochemical, biomechanical pharmacological approach to healing that ultimately seeks to "attack" disease, "combat" illness, and wage "war on cancer" or on the human body itself. This paradigm can be invaluable in emergency medicine and help us survive certain infectious diseases, but for the large majority of people facing day-to-day chronic illnesses, it provides short-term results, serious side effects, and stratospherically high costs.

The vast majority of drugs have a quick turnover in the medical marketplace, making them more akin to fashion than science. Despite this recurrent pattern, doctors are prescribing drugs at record-breaking rates. Polypharmacy (the use of more than one drug concurrently for a patient) is becoming routine, even though there is very little evidence for the safety or efficacy of such practice. Some scary details about the serious problems that result from polypharmacy was discussed in an earlier article.

The primary reason that modern medicine fails so many times is that it tends to assume that symptoms are just something "wrong" with the person that then needs to be managed, controlled, or suppressed. Distinct from this medical viewpoint is an ancient and futuristic model that recognizes that symptoms represent DEFENSES of the body that should be nurtured and augmented as a way to treat disease processes. This latter approach to treating the sick is the naturopathic and homeopathic models of the West, the ayurvedic approach of India, and the various styles of acupuncture from the East.

One hopes that the American public would greatly benefit from receiving the "best" and certainly most expensive care that modern medicine has to offer. However, this simply isn't true. In fact, the following statistics powerfully state the results from what some people mistakenly refer to as the "best" medical care in the world:

- According to 2006 data, the infant mortality rate in the United States was ranked twenty-first in the world, worse than South Korea and Greece and only slightly better than Poland.

- Data from 2006 also showed that the life expectancy rate in the United States was ranked seventeenth in the world, tied with Cyprus and only slightly ahead of Albania.

Even "Good" Research Is Often Bad

Medications that can allay pain or any type of serious discomfort are a great blessing, but let's not fool ourselves into believing that modern pain drugs are curative agents. In fact, although they provide blessed short-term relief, they create their own pathology, addiction, and demand for increasing doses over time.

Such pain relief is akin to unscrewing a warning light in your car. It does turn off that irritating light, though it does nothing to change the underlying problem.

However, when a drug company's scientific trial "proves" that their drug reduces pain, it then markets this treatment as "scientifically proven" and is able to sell the drug to doctors and to consumers with a marketable spin that makes them the big bucks. What is so brilliant about the cozy relationship that drug companies have with "science" is that most people have insurance these days and don't have to pay out of pocket for these "proven" drugs. Even though their (and our) insurance premiums skyrocket, many employers distance the patient from the real costs of paying the bill.

It is so impressive how proving that one can use conventional drugs to "unscrew a warning light" can make big big bucks. My previous article noted that the combined profits ($35.9 billion) of the ten largest drug companies in the Fortune 500 in 2002 were more than the combined profits ($33.7 billion) of the remaining 490 companies together. *In a civilized world, no industry should have this amount of profit without being considered a criminal enterprise.*

And let's also not fool ourselves into believing that conventional medical treatment is the sole method of providing pain relief. Back in 1983, I coined the term "medical chauvinism" as a common assumption that there is only one type of education with which to learn the science and art of healing or that there is only one type of health professional suitable to provide health care. Despite its recent prevalence, medical chauvinism is an anomaly historically and internationally.

Equally problematic to medical chauvinism is "scientism," which is the common assumption that science is the only way to acquire knowledge about reality. There is a great amount of human experience that cannot be tested in a "double-blind and placebo-controlled trial," and the lack of "scientific evidence" for these experiences does not make them invalid, unproven, or nonexistent.

It is more than a tad ironic that there are extremely few double-blind and placebo-controlled trials testing surgical procedures, and yet, physicians and skeptics do not refer to surgery as "quackery." Surgeons appropriately note that it is impossible to conduct such studies because it is unethical to open up a patient for surgery to provide a "placebo surgery." And yet, these same physicians and skeptics use this offensive term, "quackery," with regularity and without parity, to a host of alternative therapies that have similar challenges to providing placebo treatment. How does one give a placebo meditation, and how can many naturopathic protocols be tested

Clinical Studies Have Proven Homeopathy's Effectiveness

Homeopaths point to the nearly two hundred years of clinical experience of convinced doctors and satisfied patients. Homeopathic remedies are believed to be effective in treating a wide variety of illnesses: infectious diseases such as flu and colds; chronic conditions such as allergies, asthma, migraines, and PMS [premenstrual syndrome]. Conventional medicine has not had much success in treating many of these conditions.

Several clinical studies exist that show the effectiveness of homeopathic remedies. Many of these studies employed double-blind studies, accepted by scientists. Recent clinical trials suggest that homeopathic medicines have a positive effect on allergic rhinitis, asthma, treatment of dermatological complaints, fibrositis, influenza, and for the treatment of migraines.

"Homeopathic Medicine: Clinical Studies,"
Holisticonline.com, 2011. www.holisticonline.com.

when the combined treatment regimen includes an herb, a vitamin, a homeopathic medicine, AND some type of physical therapy.

Scientism is a type of fundamentalism where science is the religion. A significant problem with scientism is that its believers are often even more arrogant than religious fundamentalists. Perhaps worse, they don't even acknowledge that their belief system is a belief system. This problem may explain the lack of humility of many doctors and scientists.

Understanding and Rewriting History

"Who controls the past controls the future: who controls the present controls the past."

George Orwell, author of 1984

History provides us with diverse evidence about our past, but ultimately, only a small portion is told in history books. The interpretation of our past and the select use of facts and figures influence our understanding of what happened.

Historians commonly remark that whichever country wins a war or whichever worldview dominates another, the history is told through that country's perspective or that dominant point of view. This is certainly true in the history of medicine. For instance, medical historians commonly portray conventional medical practice of the past as barbaric and dangerous, and yet they have asserted that today's medical care is at the apex of "scientific medicine." The assertion that today's medical care is "proven" is a consistently repeated mantra.

History also tends to portray those who lose a war and who represent a minority point of view as having less than positive attributes. For instance, those physicians practicing medicine differently than the orthodox medical practice might be called cranks, crackpots and quacks. Such name-calling is a wonderfully clever way to trivialize potentially valuable contributions, whether or not one understands what these contributions really are.

Besides name-calling, practitioners of the conventional and dominating paradigm often spin facts to make the strong and solid features of a minority practice into something strange and weird. Homeopaths are accused of using smaller doses than used in orthodox medicine, and this is portrayed as homeopaths using doses that "theoretically" could not have any physiological effect. The medical fundamentalists purposefully ignore the significant literature that posits different theories about how homeopathic medicines work, and they (again) show their lack of humility because there are innumerable conventional medical treatments today for which the mechanism of action remains unknown. Even good skeptics know that we still do not understand how tobacco smoking causes cancer, and yet, no one advocates that we ignore this good health information just because the precise mechanism remains a mystery.

Accusations that homeopathic medicines could not possibly have any effect are made without knowledge, experience, or humility. Such accusations simply become evidence of the accuser's unscientific attitude and his or her ignorance of the diverse body of basic scientific work on the effects of nano-doses of certain substances in specific situations.

The fact that homeopaths have used their medicines for more than 200 years is spun as evidence that this system of medicine has not "progressed." Another interpretation here is that the same homeopathic medicines used 200 years ago are still used today, along with hundreds of new ones, primarily because the old ones still work. The art of using homeopathic medicines is that they are not prescribed for a localized disease but for a syndrome or pattern of symptoms of which the localized disease is a part. It is clever how some people try to spin positive attributes in hyper-negative ways.

The fact that homeopaths interview a patient to discover his or her unique symptoms has been spun to make homeopathy seem like a quirky system that revels in inane facts about a patient. However, the detailed symptoms and characteristics of the patient that homeopaths collect may not be comprehended by those unfamiliar with the unique and critical nature of individualizing features in each person. Homeopathy provides a sophisticated method by which a patient's characteristics are applied to selecting and prescribing the most effective homeopathic medicine. Today, a large majority of practicing homeopaths use expert system software to help them prescribe their medicines in a highly individualized way to patients.

Homeopaths use the term "vital force" in a fashion similar to how acupuncturists use the term "chi" to refer to the underlying forces in a living system that connects mind and body. Although antagonists to these systems of natural medicine try to make them sound "woo-woo," homeopaths and acupuncturists confidently respond by asserting that living systems are not machines or simply bodies of chemical interactions.

I personally have no problem with "skeptics" of homeopathy, though most people who think of themselves as skeptics are really simply "deniers" or "medical fundamentalists." A skeptic is one who may not believe that homeopathy works, but che (my preferred alternative to s/he) strives to be familiar with the body of literature, not just the "negative" trials. Further, a good skeptic evaluates clinical trials, basic science trials, animal studies, cost-effectiveness comparisons, outcome studies, consecutive case reports, and epidemiological data. A good skeptic is simply a good scientist who evaluates a whole body of evidence.

Sadly, most deniers of homeopathy simply and directly lie about the subject. They commonly assert that "there is no research on homeopathy" or "there is no possible mechanism of action for how homeopathic medicines work." These fundamentalists KNOW that this is not true. Several of my previous articles have referenced this body of evidence.

Some of the most recent reviews of research include one meta-analysis of clinical research published in the prestigious *Journal of Clinical Epidemiology* and two full issues of the peer-review journal *Homeopathy*, which reviewed basic sciences research.

What is so interesting to watch is the questionably honest or ethical behavior of these medical fundamentalists. They have been informed of the many studies and meta-analyses that have verified the clinical efficacy of homeopathic medicines as well as hundreds of basic sciences trials, many of which have been replicated by other researchers. One review of replications of basic science work is of special interest.

The deniers of homeopathy love to say that homeopaths "cherry-pick" the positive studies and ignore the negative ones. They then incredulously assert that we should ignore ALL of the positive trials. Such statements and viewpoints are profoundly misguided and simply daft. Will these same people say that Thomas Edison "cherry-picked" his positive study and ignored all of his "negative" studies in his efforts to invent electric lights? The (il)logic of the deniers is that they would recommend ignoring Edison's discovery because the vast majority of his studies were not positive.

Finally, medical history sheds light on what is and isn't real.

In 1832, the esteemed founder of homeopathy, Samuel Hahnemann, MD, was granted honorary membership in the Medical Society of the City and County of New York. And yet, 11 years later, the minutes of this medical society confirm that once this conventional medical association recognized the "major ideological and financial threat" that the growth of homeopathy represented, the medical society rescinded his membership. It is the ideological and financial threat that homeopathy poses that motivates the antagonism to it, not whether it works or not.

In light of the fact that history tends to be written by the victors, this writer predicts that history will soon be rewritten.

| "Homeopathy is biologically implausible, its own predictions seem to be incorrect, and the clinical evidence is largely negative."

Homeopathic Medicine Is Ineffective

Edzard Ernst

Edzard Ernst is a medical doctor who trained in several alternative medicine modalities, including acupuncture and homeopathy, and was named the first professor of complementary medicine at the University of Exeter in 1993. He is an outspoken critic of alternative medicine, the founder and editor in chief of the medical journal Focus on Alternative and Complementary Therapies, *the coauthor of* Trick or Treatment?: Alternative Medicine on Trial, *and the editor of* Healing, Hype, or Harm?: A Critical Analysis of Complementary or Alternative Medicine. *In the following viewpoint, Ernst rejects any claims or evidence purporting that homeopathy is an effective treatment for disease. He argues that modern scientific advances and research have proven that not only are the very premises upon which*

Edzard Ernst, excerpt from "The Truth About Homeopathy," *British Journal of Clinical Pharmacology*, vol. 65, no. 2, 2007, pp. 163–64. Copyright © 2007 by John Wiley & Sons. All rights reserved. Reproduced by permission. onlinelibrary.wiley.com/doi/10.1111/j.1365-2125.2007.03007.x/abstract.

homeopathy is based are inaccurate, but also the outcomes pre-dicted by homeopaths have consistently failed to materialize. The research clearly indicates, according to Ernst, that homeopathic remedies are entirely ineffective and that any perceived benefits from homeopathic treatment are purely imagined and can be at-tributed to the placebo effect.

As you read, consider the following questions:

1. What, according to Ernst, are the two main axioms of homeopathy?

2. What research findings does Ernst report regarding ho-meopathic aggravations?

3. Who conducted and then suppressed the results of a comprehensive research program on homeopathy, ac-cording to Ernst?

In this issue [of the *British Journal of Clinical Pharmacology*], [A.] Paris *et al.* report a clinical trial showing that home-opathy is not better than placebo in reducing morphine con-sumption after surgery. Proponents of homeopathy would ob-ject to this statement. Even though the study was well-made, it did only suggest that a certain homeopathic remedy fails to be effective for a certain type of pain. Other homeopathic medi-cines might be effective and other types of pain might have produced different results. There are hundreds of different ho-meopathic remedies which can be prescribed for thousands of symptoms in dozens of different dilutions. Thus we would probably need to work flat out for several lifetimes in order to arrive at a conclusion that fully substantiates my opening statement.

This seems neither possible nor desirable. Perhaps it is preferable to simply combine common sense with the best ex-isting knowledge. These two tell us that 1) homeopathy is biologically implausible, 2) its own predictions seem to be incorrect and 3) the clinical evidence is largely negative. Let me explain.

The Science Behind Homeopathy Is Flawed or Nonexistent

The main axioms of homeopathy are that 1) 'like can be cured with like' and that 2) less is more. According to the first axiom, a substance that causes certain symptoms in healthy volunteers is a cure for such symptoms in patients. The 'less is more' axiom posits that, if we dilute and shake a remedy, it becomes not weaker but stronger. The process is therefore aptly called 'potentation' by homeopaths. Homeopaths believe that the most potent remedies are those that have been potentized to the point where no 'active' molecule is left. Samuel Hahnemann, the father of homeopathy, might be forgiven for developing these concepts some 200 years ago. Today, however, we know a lot more, and comprehend that they are not in line with much that science has taught us. Yet today's followers of Hahnemann's doctrines seem to prefer mystical thinking to science.

Even homeopathy's own predictions seem to be incorrect. In order to know which remedy is effective in which situation and to apply the law of similars, homeopaths need to test each of their medicines on healthy volunteers and minutely record the symptoms it may cause. This process is called 'proving'. During the last 200 years, many such provings have been reported. A remedy is given to a group of volunteers who then record their experience. One may well ask whether the results are reliable. One could, for instance, investigate whether the symptoms reported are different from those caused by a placebo. Assessing the totality of these provings in a systematic review, homeopaths were recently surprised to find that 'the central question of whether homeopathic medicines in high dilutions can provoke effects in healthy volunteers has not yet been definitively answered'.

Homeopathy Does Not Work

The fact is, when you turn on an intact and properly functioning lightbulb, it illuminates. Every. Single. Time. The magic potions of homeopathy do not even come close to this sort of success.

PalMD, "Homeopath Dana Ullman Is an Idiot (in My Humble Opinion)," The White Coat Underground, April 30, 2010. http://scienceblogs.com.

Another prediction homeopaths believe in is that of homeopathic aggravations. These are acute exacerbations of the patient's presenting symptoms after receiving the optimal remedy. Homeopaths expect these phenomena to occur in ~20% of all patients. When we scrutinized placebo-controlled trials of homeopathy, however, we found that aggravations did not occur more frequently in the verum [group that received the treatment] than in the control group [group that received no treatment]. The likely explanation seems to be that this prediction is based on a myth.

Research Shows Clearly That Homeopathy Does Not Work

The acid test, of course, is a clinical trial of the type conducted by Paris *et al.* Is the patients' response to homeopathy truly more than a placebo effect? Many investigators have asked that crucial question. As one might expect, the answers are far from uniform. Some trials are negative, some are positive, but very few are rigorous. In this situation, it would be foolish to rely on the results of just one or two studies. What is needed is a systematic review of all studies of acceptable methodological quality. Dozens of such reviews are available today. The vast majority of those that are rigorous conclude that homeopathic medicines fail to generate clinical effects that are different from those of placebos.

Yet many patients swear by homeopathy and homeopaths insist they witness therapeutic success every day of their professional lives. The discrepancy between the trial and the observational data continues to be hotly debated. Personally, I find this somewhat puzzling. The explanation seems obvious: Patients often do improve for a number of reasons unrelated to any specific effect of the treatment we prescribe. Amongst all the placebos that exist, homeopathy has the potential to be an exceptionally powerful one—think, for instance, of the individualized remedies or the long and empathic encounter between patient and therapist.

So the conundrum of homeopathy seems to be solved. 'Heavens!' I hear the homeopathic fraternity shout. 'We need more research!' But are they correct? How much research is enough to show that any treatment does not work (sorry, is not superior to placebo)? Here we go full circle: Should we really spend several lifetimes in order to arrive at a more robust conclusion?

Perhaps one should ask the proponents of homeopathy and the best minds in medical research to design a comprehensive but finite research programme to determine the truth. As long as both camps agree at the outset to accept the results, this might be a feasible way of ending a 200-year-old dispute. Most readers and even many homeopaths will be surprised to learn that that has already happened! During the Third Reich the (mostly pro-homeopathy) Nazi leadership wanted to solve the homeopathy question once and for all. The research programme was carefully planned and rigorously executed. A report was written and it even survived the war. But it disappeared nevertheless—apparently in the hands of German homeopaths. Why? According to a very detailed eyewitness report, they were wholly and devastatingly negative.

"*What's 'working' here is everything* around *the acupuncture. . . . The improvement owes* nothing at all *to the 'traditional' mechanisms of acupuncture.*"

Sham Acupuncture's Effectiveness Casts Doubt on the Efficacy of Real Acupuncture

Ted Burnham

Ted Burnham is a graduate student at the University of Colorado Boulder, where he is pursuing a master's degree in journalism, and is a contributor to the weekly science program How On Earth, *which airs on the Boulder-Denver community radio station KGNU. In the following viewpoint, Burnham declares that a 2011 Swedish study showed that acupuncture was only effective as a placebo and not as an actual treatment, as was widely reported in news stories covering the study. In the study, cancer patients receiving radiation therapy were given either an acupuncture treatment using an acupuncture point that is believed to cure nausea or a faux, or "sham," acupuncture-like treatment that used a different point and did not pierce the skin. Patients who received either acupuncture or the faux, acupuncture-like treatment reported significantly less nausea than those who did not have either treatment. Burnham cites the authors of the study themselves as supporting his view that the patients experienced a reduction in their nausea because they believed that the acupuncture would work and because they trusted the person who administered the treatment. Burnham blames what he views as a lack of journalistic quality brought about by economic hardships faced by newsrooms around the country for the widely reported misinterpretation of this study as evidence of acupuncture's effectiveness.*

As you read, consider the following questions:

1. How were patients kept from knowing whether they were receiving a traditional acupuncture treatment or a faux acupuncture treatment, according to Burnham?

2. What does Burnham state were the percentages of patients who experienced nausea in the acupuncture groups versus those in the group that received neither treatment?

3. What happened to patients' views of acupuncture when they experienced nausea or vomiting, according to the viewpoint?

I wrote this just a few days ago, but it looks like I've missed the boat by not publishing immediately. The misleading headlines are already appearing:

- "Afraid of needles? Poke-free acupuncture works just as well" (LiveScience)

- "Acupuncture in every form reduces nausea" (*Times of India*)

Studies Suggest That Acupuncture Is Not Effective

A previous systematic review of acupuncture trials observed that the dominant rationale for acupuncture involved the release of neurotransmitters ... but not one study proposed that these neurochemical effects depend on specific points or techniques. Other rationales ... have likewise never been linked to specific points; spinal gate-control mechanisms have been linked to innervation segments, but not to specific points. Thus, there is no scientific reason to imagine that sham acupuncture should fail to mimic true acupuncture.

These findings highlight the difficulty of conducting controlled trials of acupuncture in the absence of theories about what, exactly, one is controlling for. However, while the difficulty of performing sham acupuncture presents a challenge for research, it lowers the bar for practice. If acupuncture does not depend on specific points or techniques, it significantly simplifies practice. Because the difference between true and sham acupuncture has not been clearly demonstrated, the theoretical basis and logic for acupuncture practice and research need to be reevaluated.

Howard H. Moffet,
"Sham Acupuncture May Be as Efficacious as True Acupuncture:
A Systemic Review of Clinical Trials," Journal of Alternative
and Complementary Medicine, *vol. 15, no. 3, 2009.*

- "Simulated acupuncture can treat nausea effectively in cancer patients undergoing radiotherapy"(News-Medical).

Mark my words: That is *NOT* what the data show. A more accurate headline would read:

Real acupuncture no more effective than placebo treatment.

But before you get all up in arms about the sorry state of science journalism, let me assure you that it's not really the reporters' or editors' fault. At least, not completely. In this case, the *press release itself* uses misleading language, with a headline claiming that "Acupuncture is equally effective with simulated needles." So the average journalist should be forgiven for thinking that this study supports the validity of acupuncture—which it most certainly does not.

So what's the real story?

Swedish Study Does Not Prove Acupuncture Is Effective

A new [2011] study from Karolinska Institute in Sweden used acupuncture as a treatment to reduce nausea in cancer patients undergoing radiation therapy. All patients received standard nausea-reducing drugs called "antiemetics."

In addition, about half of the patients were given a simple acupuncture treatment several times a week. This involved having a short needle poked into their skin just above their wrists, at an acupuncture point traditionally believed to reduce nausea.

The other half of the patients received a similar treatment on the same schedule, but the needles were placed several inches away from the traditional acupuncture point and did not penetrate the skin. Patients couldn't tell which group they were in because the needles were encased in opaque sheaths, and the pricking sensation on the skin was basically identical.

The patients were asked daily about their experience of nausea, their expectations that the acupuncture treatment would work, and how likely they thought they were to feel nauseated in the first place. Their responses were compared to a reference group of other radiation therapy patients—not a "control group" in the strictest sense, but similar—who were treating their nausea only with antiemetic drugs.

Patients in both the "real" and "fake" acupuncture group were less likely to experience nausea than those in the reference group. Significantly less likely, in fact—in each acupuncture group only 37% of patients reported nausea, compared to 63% of patients in the reference group.

Cue the misrepresentational headlines: *"Real AND fake acupuncture outperform standard medical care!"*

But in fact, the study's authors are quite clear that *acupuncture itself probably has nothing to do with the results.*

That's because acupuncture, as traditionally defined, makes two claims:

1. It matters where you put the needles;

2. The needles need to break the skin.

In the "fake" acupuncture group, the needles were NOT placed at the traditional nausea-reducing acupuncture point; NOR did the needles break the patients' skin. Yet the "fake" group received just as much benefit as the "real" group did.

Conclusion: Neither of the mechanisms claimed by acupuncture is responsible for the benefit the patients received.

Anna Enblom, the lead author of the study, speculated on the many other factors that could have produced a positive outcome for these patients (in this passage, "verum" means "real", "sham" means "fake", and "emesis" means "nausea"):

> The verum and the sham group received extra care compared to the standard care group, which may have reduced emesis: patient-therapist communication, the knowledge that continuous contact with one single therapist would continue during the whole radiotherapy period, the tactile stimulation from the therapists' hands, the extra time for rest and relaxation and the extra attention to the patient's symptoms through the daily emesis questions all are important elements of this extra care.

In other words, *what helped these patients was that they received extra attention from a trusted medical professional, in a relaxing, reassuring and empathetic setting.* And that could just as easily be accomplished without using needles or targeting special points on the body.

Acupuncture's Benefits Are Due to the Placebo Effect and Nothing More

Another factor was that most of the patients expected their acupuncture treatment to be effective. That's part of the placebo effect: A patient thinks she's getting a real treatment, so her brain tricks itself into feeling like her symptoms are relieved. It works with mild symptoms, but—as Enblom points out here—"if a noxious stimulation is performed after taking a placebo pill, the study subject no longer believes in the effect of the placebo pill." And indeed, patients who experienced nausea or vomiting were more likely to lose trust in acupuncture.

So, what this study really tells us is:

"Real" acupuncture is itself a placebo treatment.

What's frustrating about this is that, when studied this way, acupuncture does produce better outcomes . . . because it is a) an extra intervention that b) patients tend to believe will be effective.

That sounds an awful lot like saying that acupuncture "works"—but that would be the wrong interpretation. What's "working" here is everything *around* the acupuncture: The fact that *any* intervention is taking place, and the fact that the patients trust the person doing it. The improvement owes *nothing at all* to the "traditional" mechanisms of acupuncture.

The acupuncture is acting as a placebo—a stand-in that allows all of the *elements* of treatment to come into play, without actually *being* a treatment. Once again:

Acupuncture is a placebo. That's ALL it is.

Substandard Journalism
Perpetuates Misconceptions

Unfortunately we've seen this sort of misreporting before. There have been a number of studies that have taken this "Wrong place, fake needle" approach to studying acupuncture and come to similar conclusions. Invariably, they are reported by many major news outlets with the emphasis entirely backwards—"Acupuncture—real or fake—best for back pain" (MSNBC)—although there are a few places that do a proper job—"Fake acupuncture as good as 'real' acupuncture" (About.com). (I do take issue with the About.com headline; while the use of scare quotes around 'real' makes an ironic jab at the issue, I'd rather see a strong statement about the lack of efficacy—"as good as" confuses the issue.)

It seems to me that this nonsense is one of the drawbacks of press-release journalism, which is becoming ever more popular as newsroom budgets are slashed and dedicated specialist reporters (like science writers) are laid off. If the media relations folks writing the press releases don't represent the research honestly, misconceptions are going to spread far and fast.

I can't really blame someone working for a for-profit company if they try to spin their press releases as positively as they can—the system is set up to give them a compelling reason to do so. But at a scientific institution, where the goal is supposed to be the pursuit of truth and the spreading of knowledge, this kind of thing seems counterintuitive.

| "The methods utilized in most acupuncture research are, without question, a 'sham.'"

Acupuncture Is Effective Despite Research Showing That Sham Acupuncture Is Helpful

John Amaro

John Amaro is a chiropractor, acupuncturist, practitioner of Chinese medicine, lecturer, and author of many articles on acupuncture and Chinese medicine. In the following viewpoint, Amaro rejects the results of scientific studies that indicate that faux, or "sham," acupuncture is as effective as traditional acupuncture or that acupuncture's benefits are limited to a placebo effect. Amaro contends that superficial needle stimulation has long been a widely used treatment modality within acupuncture, in which traditional acupuncture points are stimulated, patients' energy pathways are still affected, and patients still experience the sensation of needle insertion; however, in research studies this legitimate technique is misused and misinterpreted as "fake" acu-

John Amaro, "Real vs. 'Sham' Acupuncture: Challenging Recent Negative Research," *Dynamic Chiropractic*, September 9, 2009. Copyright © 2009 by MPA Media. All rights reserved. Reproduced by permission.

puncture. Amaro points out the flaws in research studies of acupuncture, illustrating the errors made in using incorrect acupuncture techniques, points, and a lack of understanding of basic principles and methods involved in acupuncture. Amaro concludes that the results of studies of acupuncture that are conducted without using proper techniques or even a basic understanding of acupuncture are invalid and should not be used to determine acupuncture's effectiveness.

As you read, consider the following questions:

1. What are special sham acupuncture needles called, according to Amaro?

2. Where was funding received for the arm-pain study conducted by researchers from Harvard Medical School, according to the viewpoint?

3. Of what four acupuncture techniques does Amaro indicate the researchers conducting the study of acupuncture's effectiveness as a treatment for colitis never heard?

When a 2005 research article in *JAMA* [*Journal of the American Medical Association*] reported, "Acupuncture treatment no more effective than sham treatment in reducing migraine headache," it raised doubts in the minds of the general public and the medical/scientific community as to acupuncture's efficacy. This year, the online science news journal *ScienceDaily* printed what appeared to be a continuation of that study. The article was titled "Acupuncture Stops Headaches, but 'Faked' Treatments Work Almost as Well." This particular report was picked up by the international news and reported as a statement of fact that acupuncture was a questionable modality, especially regarding the application by professional practitioners. It was emphatically questioned whether "better trained acupuncturists really achieve better results than those with basic training only."

Superficial Needling Is a Legitimate Practice Within Acupuncture

True needling consists of actual penetration of the needle with manual stimulation, whereas sham needling is carried out by a special needle that touches the skin but may only penetrate superficially or touch the skin's surface. In cases of both true and sham, the *de qi* phenomenon [connection between needles and energy pathways] is reported and the subject feels the needle at the point of contact.

Superficial needle stimulation is a known and accepted acupuncture procedure within a variety of European and Asian American acupuncture techniques. Within acupuncture research, however, it is considered a placebo. Conclusions will be drawn and reported as such to an unsuspecting public. These sham acupuncture needles, which are internationally accepted and referred to as Streitberger . . . needles, are used by virtually every researcher conducting studies within the area of acupuncture. It is the standard for the scientific industry. This fact alone makes any research using this needle procedure a "sham," as it ignores that non-penetrating acupuncture is a valid technique.

Studies of Acupuncture Are Poorly Designed and Executed

But that hasn't stopped the research. Also this year [2009], the *Journal of Alternative and Complementary Medicine* reported the results of a study titled "Sham Acupuncture May Be as Efficacious as True Acupuncture: A Systematic Review of Clinical Trials." The conclusion was: "The findings cast doubt on the validity of traditional acupuncture theories about point locations and indications . . . and the theoretical basis for traditional acupuncture practice needs to be reevaluated."

In this particular study, studies were categorized by use of wrong points, nonpoints, and normal insertion and stimulation versus superficial insertion or minimal stimulation. The researchers obviously discounted superficial stimulation, as in various forms of Japanese acupuncture, as a valid treatment despite its thousand-plus-year history. They further discounted any acupuncture points as invalid or wrong other than those illustrated on the human acupuncture mannequin or a typical acupuncture chart.

The *Clinical Journal of Pain* reported on "Acupuncture for treatment of persistent arm pain due to repetitive use" last year. The study was conducted by researchers from Harvard Medical School, among others, and funded by a grant from the National Center for Complementary and Alternative Medicine. The study objective was: "to compare true and sham acupuncture in their abilities to relieve arm pain and function." The conclusion of the study was: "Arm pain scores improved in both groups during the treatment period, but improvements were significantly greater in the sham group than in the true acupuncture group. The true acupuncture group experienced more side effects, predominately mild pain at time of treatments."

Overall, this study did not find evidence to support the effectiveness of true acupuncture in treatment of persistent arm pain. Sham acupuncture and true acupuncture achieved similar response, with the possibility of sham acupuncture being more effective. This particular research relied on a "manualized" approach, meaning a cookbook procedure for arm pain with the addition of all participants receiving needling (sham or true) to LIV (LR) 3 on the contralateral side and LI 4 on the side of pain. Non-meridian local points (*ah shi*), which researchers discount as being nonpoints, were included in the study.

A consensus team of "senior acupuncturists" selected 20 allowable acupuncture points based upon a manualized approach. The researchers obviously felt this gave them acceptability within the scientific community as a valid source, as certain acupuncture prescriptions have been printed and published. The sources of these formulas, however, are unknown. Practitioners could select no more than eight additional points at each treatment and could include local area points traditionally used to affect specific regions (LI 5, P 5, P 6, P 7 and TW 5) and local and distal sensitive *ah shi* points. No other specific points were allowed in the research. Why these specific points were chosen remains a question of considerable merit.

Research Studies Reveal Ignorance About Acupuncture

Recently, a major research institute attached to a very prominent university received a grant to conduct acupuncture research. They chose as their topic the treatment of colitis and diverticulitis via acupuncture. They sought my input and expertise into the matter. To say I was honored and humbled would be an understatement. When I inquired as to my role, I was shocked to learn they wanted to know, "What points do you treat for this condition?"

They did not have a clue what acupuncture was. They only wanted to know what points to use for gastrointestinal distress. I reminded them that was a very general condition with many potential causes. I advised against using federal funds to finance such a study since their final results would be flawed. They were totally unaware of pulse, tongue diagnosis, system review or electro-meridian imaging through *ryodoraku* [a Japanese form of acupuncture involving ryodo points, which are very close to traditional acupuncture points]. When I asked what their goal for the research was, I was told: "To determine if acupuncture was effective in gastrointestinal distress."

It is very apparent that those who are conducting what would otherwise be considered valid and scientific research at extremely impressive and recognized institutes are in fact guilty of the highest malfeasance with the models they have chosen to use regarding the effectiveness of acupuncture. Unfortunately, the general public and the scientific community regard research from these sources as gospel and would never question the validity of these studies. Acupuncture research conclusions cannot be accepted as long as the research is being conducted as shown in the examples I cited. True blind or double-blind studies comparing needle and sham treatment may essentially be impossible within acupuncture research due to the fact that as long as a patient is able to feel a sensation at the point of needle contact (whether actual or simulated), it cannot be considered a valid blind study. Thus, it is my opinion that the methods utilized in most acupuncture research are, without question, a "sham."

"*Opponents of chelation have published several sham studies, in an attempt to show that EDTA chelation does not work. In every instance the actual data from those studies showed benefit, but the authors published deceptive erroneous conclusions.*"

Chelation Therapy Is a Safe and Effective Treatment for Many Conditions

Elmer M. Cranton

Elmer M. Cranton is a board certified medical doctor; a graduate of Harvard Medical School; a charter fellow of the American Academy of Family Physicians; and the author of several books and articles on chelation therapy, antiaging and preventive medicine, and nutrition, including A Textbook on EDTA Chelation Therapy. *In the following viewpoint, Cranton refutes the claims made by Saul Green on the website Quackwatch about chelation therapy, which is the intravenous injection of chelating agents—substances like ethylenediaminetetraacetic acid, or EDTA. Cran-*

Elmer M. Cranton, "Busting the Quackbusters: Rebuttal to 'Quackwatch' Website Opposing Chelation Therapy," DrCranton.com, 2007. Copyright © 2007 by DrCranton .com. All rights reserved. Reproduced by permission.

ton offers evidence to contradict Green's claims that chelation therapy is ineffective, untested, illegal, unethical, and dangerous. Cranton explains that the research data cited by Green is misrepresented, and furthermore that drug manufacturing companies and cardiovascular health care providers have a vested interest in denying the effectiveness of chelation therapy, since it would significantly reduce their profits from the sale of cardiac medications and from performing expensive procedures such as bypass surgery and balloon angioplasty. Cranton maintains that studies that show positive outcomes for chelation therapy in the treatment of heart disease and other health conditions are routinely misreported as negative outcomes to preserve the status quo in medical care. Cranton rejects the notion that chelation therapy is an unproven treatment performed by unscientific practitioners, and he offers research study results to support his claims of chelation therapy's effectiveness.

As you read, consider the following questions:

1. Why does Cranton say that double-blind studies, like those performed by drug companies on new drugs, have not been done on EDTA chelation therapy?

2. According to *BusinessWeek* statistics cited by Cranton, how many bypass surgeries and angioplasties are performed each year?

3. According to Cranton, the average walking distance of patients in the Curt Diehm study in Germany increased by what percentage following EDTA chelation therapy?

A small number of self-styled medical thought-police call themselves "quack busters." They attack chelation [the intravenous injection of chelating agents into the blood stream] and other alternative, innovative and leading-edge medical therapies in favor of the existing medical monopoly. They have their own Quackwatch Internet website. Who are these so-called quackbusters, who funds them? It would be interesting [to] uncover the financial backing for this group. Who pays for this type of attack on competing therapies? It has been alleged that funding comes indirectly, through a number of cutouts, from a consortium of pharmaceutical manufacturers.

In past years the so-called quackbusters have attacked nutritional supplementation and high-potency multivitamins as "quackery." As summarized on this website, recent scientific studies now prove that virtually anyone could benefit from nutritional supplementation. With egg on their faces from recent nutritional research, these "Quackbusters" continue to attack chelation therapy. [Available at the] Quackwatch website [is an] article by Dr. Saul Green entitled "Chelation Therapy: Unproven Claims and Unsound Theories." Green attempts to discredit EDTA [ethylenediaminetetraacetic acid, a chelating agent] chelation using half-truths, speculation, and false statements. Saul Green is president of ZOL Consultants, a company paid to investigate alleged health frauds. Now, who do you suppose would pay Saul Green for that? You might ask him.

Read below for a point-by-point rebuttal to this misleading article.

Critics of EDTA chelation rarely state that chelation "does not work" or that chelation is "proven not to work." Instead they state that it is "unproven" by large, FDA [US Food and Drug Administration]-approved, double-blind, placebo-controlled clinical trials. That same statement can be made about most widely approved treatments in medicine. They deceptively apply a double standard. Bypass surgery [grafting veins from other areas of the body to bypass damaged heart arteries], balloon angioplasty [opening a blocked artery by inflating a balloon inserted with a catheter through the femoral artery], and close to 80% of all therapies routinely used in medical practice are "unproven" by the same criteria.

More than 80% of widely accepted and traditional medical therapies have never been subjected to double-blind, placebo-controlled clinical trials—as demanded by opponents of chelation therapy. Critics evasively and deceptively apply a double standard.

Detractors of chelation insist that large, multimillion-dollar studies must be performed, giving half the patients a placebo, with the placebo group "blinded"—unknown to the investigators until the study is complete (called "double-blind and placebo-controlled" because neither the doctors nor the patients know who gets the placebo and who gets the medication under study). Drug companies are required by the FDA to test new prescription drugs that way, before they can make marketing claims. On the other hand, bypass surgery, balloon angioplasty, and 80% of widely accepted medical procedures have never been subjected to that type of testing. Because patents have expired on EDTA, there is no way to recoup the cost of such a study.

There Are No Laws Against Using Chelation Therapy

Saul Green cites an FTC [US Federal Trade Commission] ruling in 1998 banning the interstate advertising of EDTA chelation therapy by a professional medical membership association. That ruling does not in any way apply to the practice of chelation therapy by clinics and health care providers. Because the FDA has not yet approved EDTA chelation therapy for treatment of atherosclerosis, the FTC ruled that it is not proper for a professional membership association to imply otherwise in advertisements to the lay public. That ruling does not apply to individual health care providers and clinics.

An informed consent provided to patients by chelation clinics has always made clear that the FDA does not endorse this off-label use. Politically powerful opponents of chelation therapy thus generated adverse publicity using what was essentially a nonissue.

Drug companies patent new drugs to allow them to charge high prices (usually a dollar or more per dose, sometimes much more) to recapture the millions of dollars it costs for FDA-required double-blind studies. EDTA is a generic drug and patent protection expired many years ago.

Scientific Studies Show Positive Results for Chelation Therapy

Many smaller studies have been published documenting the benefits of EDTA chelation therapy, with data showing objective measurements of before and after improvement. Statistical analyses of those improvements are highly significant. . . . A chapter from the book *Bypassing Bypass Surgery* summarizes a large amount of research and clinical studies supporting EDTA chelation therapy. Every published study of chelation therapy has been positive, with data showing benefit (although several studies have misrepresented that positive data).

The studies that support EDTA chelation are scientifically valid, even though they are not placebo controlled. Only if it is assumed that placebo effect could cause long-term, sustained increases in objective blood flow measurements to the brain, heart, and extremities through diseased arteries can those studies be ignored. Placebo effect has never been observed to last more than 6 months. Benefit from chelation therapy comes on slowly, not peaking until 3 or more months after treatment is complete and persisting for years after a course of therapy. Placebo benefit occurs immediately and has never been reported to last 6 months.

Saul Green's quackbuster attack on chelation therapy states that published studies are poorly designed and therefore meaningless. Any educated lay reader will be impressed with the data in those studies. It is always desirable to have bigger and better studies. There is always room for improvement. That same statement could be made about any study ever published. The existing clinical data is all positive and highly significant on statistical analysis. Independent researchers, at different research facilities, using different technology, have been able to duplicate the beneficial findings of increased blood flow through blocked arteries. . . .

Study Results Are Manipulated to Protect Cardiovascular Care Industry Profits

According to *BusinessWeek*, doctors are doing about 400,000 bypass surgeries and 1 million angioplasties a year—a heart surgery industry worth an estimated $100 billion a year. The cardiovascular drug industry takes in upwards of another $100 billion per year. If the clinical studies of chelation therapy were accepted as valid, those industries would suffer enormous losses. They have no reason to want to see chelation therapy accepted.

Opponents of chelation have published several sham studies, in an attempt to show that EDTA chelation does not work. In every instance the actual data from those studies showed benefit, but the authors published deceptive erroneous conclusions.

The so-called PATCH study performed in Calgary, Canada, is a blatant example of such a practice and represents a kind of junk science that proves nothing. It actually contains evidence to support EDTA chelation therapy, despite a deceptively negative conclusion. Such studies are quickly published in mainstream medical journals, interspersed with full-page, four-color advertisements for new and expensive pharmaceutical drugs. The news media report that EDTA chelation therapy has been proven not to work. Few readers take the time to carefully analyze the data to arrive at their own unbiased conclusions.

The informed consumer should review all available sources of information and then make up his or her own mind about what is best. Study all the facts and decide what feels right, without being subjected to the "time-bomb-in-chest" hard-sell for bypass surgery or angioplasty at a time when you are frightened and highly vulnerable. Treadmills and angiograms can be very effective marketing tools for expensive, dangerous, and often unnecessary therapies.

Mark Twain once wrote, "If the only tool you have is a hammer, everything looks like a nail." A similar statement could be made about cardiologists, whose favored tool is a catheter with balloon or stent attached, or surgeons and their scalpels. The same might also be said of a chelation therapist. Buyer beware! Be an informed consumer. Every therapist has their own bias.

Saul Green writes that the [J. Roderick] Kitchell, [Lawrence E.] Meltzer reappraisal study in 1963 showed no significant benefit. The opposite is true. The data from that study is carefully presented and analyzed on [our website]. Decide for yourself if you think that study shows significant benefit. For political, economic, and other unknown reasons, researchers often interpret their data to fit their personal prejudices, either positive or negative. An unbiased and objective appraisal of that same data may indicate an opposite conclusion. This has occurred repeatedly with chelation therapy. Studies have been stated by the researchers themselves as having been designed at the outset to discredit chelation therapy. Results are then interpreted to support that position.

Chelation Has Support Within the Medical Community and Patients Show Improvement

Saul Green writes that chelation is "not recognized by the scientific community." That is not true unless it is assumed that the many highly trained physicians who administer chelation

Chelation Therapy Promotes Health and Healing

Chelation therapy is a safe, effective and relatively inexpensive treatment to restore blood flow in victims of atherosclerosis without surgery and to eliminate toxins and heavy metals from your system.

Chelation therapy involves the intravenous infusion of a prescription medicine called ethylenediaminetetraacetic acid (EDTA), plus vitamins and minerals at therapeutic dosages.

EDTA chelation infusions are administered by slow drip, circulating through the bloodstream treating the entire arterial system removing undesirable metals from the body. . . . All metals, even essential nutritional elements, are toxic in excess or when abnormally situated. EDTA normalizes the distribution of most metallic elements in the body. . . .

Chelation therapy promotes health by correcting the major underlying cause of arterial blockage. Damaging oxygen-free radicals are increased by the presence of metallic elements and act as a chronic irritant to blood vessel walls and cell membranes. EDTA removes those metallic irritants, allowing leaky and damaged cell walls to heal. Plaques smooth over and shrink, allowing more blood to pass. Arterial walls become softer and more pliable, allowing easier expansion. Scientific studies have proven that blood flow increases after chelation therapy. A complete program of chelation therapy involves a broad-based care program of regular exercise, proper nutrition, vitamin and mineral supplementation and avoidance of tobacco and other damaging habits.

"Chelation Therapy," Patients Medical, 2010.
www.patientsmedical.com.

therapy are not a part of the scientific community. Doctors who disagree with Saul Green are thus labeled as unscientific.

Various segments of the medical community seem to join together in professional membership associations with one goal of protecting their turf and maintaining a monopoly in their field as much as possible. It is not justified for one such group to state that other medical scientists who disagree are "unscientific." Instead this merely represents a disagreement between experts, differing opinions of others in the medical profession—a common occurrence in any profession. Innovative complementary and alternative therapies are commonly subjected to that type of bias. (It might be mentioned that Saul Green is not a clinical practitioner with experience in chelation therapy. He is a PhD and his stated career has been in cancer research.)

Saul Green writes that at least fifteen different reports document that EDTA did not benefit patients. That is not true! For the most part, he cites letters to the editor, which report an occasional treatment failure. No therapy is 100% effective and treatment failures do occur with EDTA. However, more than 85% of patients have been helped. Anecdotal case reports of treatment failures are used by critics of chelation, but anecdotal reports of treatment success are rejected by critics—more double standard. Saul Green also misrepresents those studies previously mentioned as documenting that EDTA chelation does not work.

Arteriograms before and after treatment are demanded by critics to prove benefit from chelation therapy. It is not possible, however, to reliably measure improvements on arteriogram (also called angiogram) unless the diameter of an artery is increased by approximately 25%. With turbulent blood flow past a plaque blockage, it requires a mere 10% increase in arterial diameter to double the flow of blood (Poiseuille's law of hemodynamics as can be found in any textbook of medical physiology or biophysics). As proven in published clinical studies, arteriograms and ultrasound are not sensitive enough to consistently measure changes of less than 25% in the diameter of a blood vessel. Increases much less than that can greatly relieve or totally eliminate symptoms, and thus [may] not be detectable on arteriograms. Studies that measure heart and organ function and total blood flow consistently prove that EDTA chelation therapy is highly beneficial.

If patients improve their physical endurance, if exercise tolerance increases by objective measurement, and if symptoms improve, that in itself provides good scientific evidence of benefit. If measurements of walking distance on a treadmill with an uphill incline consistently increase after treatment and with statistical significance that is valid scientific proof of benefit. Angiograms are not sensitive enough to measure even a doubling in blood flow. Angiograms are often used as marketing tools to justify bypass surgery, stents, or balloon angioplasty; however, angiograms cannot show increases in arterial diameter that can increase blood flow by 200% or more. They do, however, show the surgeons where to cut and are necessary to place a balloon or stent in angioplasty.

Saul Green is in error when he states that the Curt Diehm study in Germany did not show benefit. The raw data from that study has been analyzed by medical school experts in the United States and was found to be highly positive, as detailed in a critique of the Heidelberg study. Patients who received EDTA increased their walking distance by an average of 400%, compared to 60% increase in the control group patients (controls actually received another type of active drug, not a placebo). The manufacturer of the control drug funded the study and reserved the right to manipulate and report the data. The patients who responded best were eliminated from the final data as "outliers." Final results were reported too soon. Three months later the improvements were much greater, as expected following EDTA. Analysis of raw data from that study proves that EDTA chelation therapy was highly effective in treating arterial blockage in the legs.

Chelation Is Significantly Safer than Surgery or Balloon Angioplasty

Potential adverse side effects described by Saul Green were reported many years ago when large overdoses of EDTA were infused in a very short time. Any medicine given in overdose can cause harm. There are no documented reports of harm when EDTA has been administered using the currently approved dose-rate protocol. In recent rare reports of adverse side effects, the approved protocol was not followed. Even when administered improperly, 10 deaths in a million patients indicate that chelation is infinitely safer than surgery or balloon angioplasty, which result in death from complications in approximately 2 out of every hundred patients treated.

Fifty thousand people die in automobile accidents every year and another 200,000 are seriously injured. The drive to the clinic in an automobile to get chelation therapy is statistically far more dangerous than the chelation they receive after they arrive. More than 8,000 deaths and 200,000 hospitalizations each year result from complications of ibuprofen, naproxen, aspirin and other widely accepted over-the-counter pain remedies. EDTA chelation therapy is infinitely safer than even those treatments.

Critics of chelation therapy rarely put things in proper perspective. Saul Green goes on to speculate about a number of theoretical reasons why chelation therapy *might* possibly be dangerous. He ignores the amazing safety record of a million patients who have received the therapy. The dangers of surgery and angioplasty are well proven, not just theoretical—two percent death rate and twenty percent or more serious but nonfatal complications. It is not necessary to merely speculate why invasive procedures might possibly cause harm. Saul

Green's statements about why chelation might be dangerous are supported after more than 40 years of experience.

The Danish study mentioned by Saul Green was misrepresented and proved nothing. It was actually a positive study and showed benefit from chelation therapy.

Saul Green states that the FDA once had EDTA chelation on their list of "[Top Ten] Health Frauds." Many years ago the FDA removed chelation therapy from that list, and for good reason. Why did they do that?

> *"The chelation 'establishment' is not being victimized by a prejudiced and arrogant medical orthodoxy but by its own unwillingness to mount a rigorous, placebo-controlled, double-blind clinical trial and stand by the results."*

Chelation Therapy Is Dangerous and Ineffective for Treating Most Health Problems

Saul Green

Saul Green was a biochemist who specialized in cancer research at Memorial Sloan-Kettering Cancer Center in New York City. In the following viewpoint, Green offers a detailed, comprehensive analysis of the efficacy of chelation therapy as a treatment for heart disease and other conditions, and he concludes that there is no clinical or scientific evidence to support its use. Green contends that the supposedly scientific body of evidence in support of chelation's health benefits offered by proponents of chelation therapy is actually a collection of erroneous conclusions

based on badly designed studies and anecdotal stories of success and endorsements from patients and chelation therapy practitioners. Green alleges that not only are chelation therapy
enthusiasts making false claims about the healing properties of
chelation, but they also are misleading the public about the
safety of what is actually a risky procedure. Green offers evidence
from double-blind, controlled, and randomized studies that found
no health benefits from chelation therapy as a treatment for atherosclerosis (heart disease caused by blocked arteries) to illustrate
his argument, and he lists various government and professional
medical organizations that have rejected chelation therapy as a
legitimate or effective medical treatment for atherosclerosis.*

As you read, consider the following questions:

1. What was the original name of the American College
   for Advancement in Medicine (ACAM) when it was
   founded in 1973, according to Green?

2. Why does Green claim that the conclusions of the 1989
   Olszewer and Carter study were not justified?

3. Why did the *FDA Consumer* remove chelation therapy
   from its October 1989 list of "Top Ten Health Frauds,"
   according to Green?

Chelation therapy, as discussed in this [viewpoint], is a series of intravenous infusions containing disodium EDTA
[ethylenediaminetetraacetic acid, a chelating agent] and various other substances. It is sometimes done by swallowing
EDTA or other agents in pill form. Proponents claim that
EDTA chelation therapy is effective against atherosclerosis
[heart disease caused by blocked arteries] and many other serious health problems. Its use is widespread because patients
have been led to believe that it is a valid alternative to established medical interventions such as coronary bypass surgery.
However, there is no scientific evidence that this is so. It is

also used to treat nonexistent "lead poisoning," "mercury poisoning," and other alleged toxic states that practitioners diagnose with tests on blood, urine, and/or hair.

The proponents' viewpoints have been summarized in four books: *The Chelation Answer: How to Prevent Hardening of the Arteries and Rejuvenate Your Cardiovascular System* (1982), by Morton Walker, D.P.M., and Garry Gordon, M.D.; *Chelation Therapy: The Key to Unclogging Your Arteries, Improving Oxygenation, Treating Vision Problems, Reversing Sexual Difficulties, Fighting Arthritis, an Alternative to Amputation* (1985), by John Parks Trowbridge, M.D., and Morton Walker D.P.M.; *A Textbook on EDTA Chelation Therapy* (1989), [edited] by Elmer M. Cranton, M.D.; and *Bypassing Bypass: The New Technique of Chelation Therapy* (2nd edition, 1990), by Elmer [M.] Cranton, M.D., and Arline Brecher. The scientific jargon in these books may create the false impression that chelation therapy for atherosclerosis, and a host of other conditions, is scientifically sound. The authors allege that between 300,000 and 500,000 patients have safely benefited. However, their evidence consists of anecdotes, testimonials, and poorly designed experiments.

This [viewpoint] identifies the major claims made for EDTA chelation and examines each in light of established scientific fact. The sources used for this review included position papers of professional societies, technical textbooks, research and review articles, newspaper articles, patient testimonials, medical records, legal depositions, transcripts of court testimony, privately published books, clinic brochures, and personal correspondence. [Note: Chelation with other substances has legitimate use in a few situations. For example, deferoxamine (desferal) is used to treat iron-overload from multiple transfusions. But this is not related to the topic of this (viewpoint), and chelation with disodium EDTA is not a substitute for desferal chelation.]

The Early History of Chelation Therapy

The term chelate, from the Greek *chele* for claw, refers to the "claw-like" structure of the organic chemical ethylenediamine-tetraacetic acid (EDTA), first synthesized in Germany in the 1930s. With this claw, EDTA binds di- and trivalent metallic ions to form a stable ring structure. EDTA is water soluble and chelates only metallic ions that are dissolved in water. At pH 7.4 (the normal pH of blood) the strength with which EDTA binds dissolved metals, in decreasing order, is: iron+++ (ferric ion), mercury++, copper++, aluminum+++, nickel++, lead++, cobalt++, zinc++, iron++ (ferrous ion), cadmium++, manganese++, magnesium++, and calcium++.

Mercury, lead, and cadmium cannot be metabolized by the body and, if accumulated, can cause toxic effects by interfering with various physiological functions. These substances are called "heavy metals," a term applied to metallic elements whose specific gravity is about 5.0 or greater, especially those that are poisonous. Except for aluminum, the other elements listed in the previous paragraph are essential nutrients that are needed for normal metabolic activity.

After EDTA was found effective in chelating and removing toxic metals from the blood, some scientists postulated that hardened arteries could be softened if the calcium in their walls was removed. The first indication that EDTA treatment might benefit patients with atherosclerosis came from [NE] Clarke, [CN] Clarke, and [RE] Mosher, who, in 1956, reported that patients with occlusive peripheral vascular disease said they felt better after treatment with EDTA.

In 1960, [Lawrence E.] Meltzer et al., who had studied ten patients with angina pectoris, reported that there was no objective evidence of improvement in any of them that could be ascribed to the course of EDTA chelation treatment. However, during the next two months, most of the patients began reporting unusual improvement in their symptoms. Prompted by these results, [J. Roderick] Kitchell et al. studied the effects of chelation on 28 additional patients and reappraised the course of the ten patients used in the original trial. They found that although 25 of the 38 patients had exhibited improved anginal patterns and half had shown improvement in electrocardiographic patterns several months after the treatment had begun, these effects were not lasting. At the time of the report, 12 of the 38 had died and only 15 reported feeling better. (This "improvement" was not significant, however, because it was no better than would be expected with proven methods and because there was no control group for comparison.) Kitchell et al. concluded that EDTA chelation, as used in this study, was "not a useful clinical tool in the treatment of coronary disease."

The "Approved" Protocol for Chelation Therapy

The primary organization promoting chelation therapy is the American College for Advancement in Medicine (ACAM), which was founded in 1973 as the American Academy [of] Medical Preventics. Since its inception, ACAM's focus has been the promotion of chelation therapy. The group conducts courses, sponsors the *Journal of Advancement in Medicine,* and administers a "board certification" program that is not recognized by the scientific community. ACAM's online directory lists about 850 members, about 550 of whom indicate that they practice chelation therapy.

In 1989, an ACAM protocol for "the safe and effective administration of EDTA chelation therapy" was included in Cranton's "textbook," a 420-page special issue of the journal that contains 28 articles and a foreword by Linus Pauling. The protocol calls for intravenous infusion of 500 to 1,000 ml [milliliters] of a solution containing 50 mg [milligrams] of disodium EDTA per kilogram of body weight, plus heparin, magnesium chloride, a local anesthetic (to prevent pain at the infusion site), several B vitamins, and 4 to 20 grams of vitamin C. This solution is infused slowly over 3.5 to 4 hours, one to three times a week. The initial recommendation is about 30 such treatments, with the possibility of additional ones later. Additional vitamins, minerals, and other substances—prescribed orally—"vary according to preferences of both patients and physicians." Lifestyle modification, which includes stress reduction, caffeine avoidance, alcohol limitation, smoking cessation, exercise, and nutritional counseling, is encouraged as part of the complete therapeutic program. The number of treatments to achieve "optimal therapeutic benefit" for patients with symptomatic disease is said to range from 20 ("minimum"), 30 (usually needed), or 40 ("not uncommon before benefit is reported") to as many as 100 or more over a period of several years. "Full benefit does not normally occur for up to 3 months after a series is completed," the protocol states—and "follow-up treatments may be given once or twice monthly for long-term maintenance, to sustain improvement and to prevent recurrence of symptoms." The cost, typically $75 to $125 per treatment, is not covered by most insurance companies. Some chelationists, in an attempt to secure coverage for their patients, misstate on their insurance claims that they are treating heavy-metal poisoning.

In 1997, ACAM issued a revised protocol describing the same procedures but adding circumstances (contraindications) under which chelation should not be performed. As in 1989, the document gives no criteria for determining: (1) who should be treated, (2) how much treatment should be given, or (3) how to tell whether the treatment is working.

Unproven Claims Made by Chelation Therapy Supporters

Proponents claim that chelation therapy is effective against atherosclerosis, coronary heart disease, and peripheral vascular disease. Its supposed benefits include increased collateral blood circulation; decreased blood viscosity; improved cell membrane function; improved intracellular organelle function; decreased arterial vasospasm; decreased free radical formation; inhibition of the aging process; reversal of atherosclerosis; decrease in angina; reversal of gangrene; improvement of skin color; and healing of diabetic ulcers. Proponents also claim that chelation is effective against arthritis; multiple sclerosis; Parkinson's disease; psoriasis; Alzheimer's disease; and problems with vision, hearing, smell, muscle coordination, and sexual potency. None of these claimed benefits has been demonstrated by well-designed clinical trials.

In a retrospective study of 2,870 patients treated with NaMgEDTA, [E.] Olszewer and [JP] Carter (1989) concluded that EDTA chelation therapy benefited patients with cardiac disease, peripheral vascular disease, and cerebrovascular disease. These conclusions were not justified because the people who received the treatment were not compared to people who did not.

In 1990, these authors carried out a "double-blind study" in which EDTA chelation was used to treat ten patients with peripheral vascular disease. The authors claimed that this was the first such study. The patients' progress was evaluated by measuring changes in their blood pressure and their performance in exercise stress tests before, during, and after the course of treatment. The authors claimed that EDTA had a significant impact on the patients' clinical status because the removal of calcium, copper, and zinc from the vascular compartment corrected cholesterol and lipoprotein metabolism; triggered a parathyroid response that pulled calcium from the bones; decreased platelet aggregation; lessened iron-generated free radical formation; reduced membrane lipid peroxidation; decreased plaque formation; and prevented intracellular calcium accumulation.

Between 1963 and 1985, independent physicians published at least fifteen separate reports documenting the case histories of more than seventy patients who had received chelation treatments. They found no evidence of change in the atherosclerotic disease process, no decrease in the size of atherosclerotic plaques, and no evidence that narrowed arteries opened wider.

More recently, the results of two randomized, controlled, double-blind clinical trials of chelation therapy were published in peer-reviewed German medical journals. The first was conducted by Curt Diehm, M.D., at the University of Heidelberg medical clinic. Diehm studied 45 patients who had intermittent claudication, a condition in which impaired circulation causes the individual to develop pain in the legs upon walking. About half of the patients were treated with EDTA and the rest received Bencyclan, a blood-thinning agent. In addition to determining the effect of each agent on the ability to perform pain-free walking exercises, Diehm measured the progress of the disease process in each patient during the four-week treatment period and three months after treatment was stopped. Statistical evaluation of the results after the blinding code was broken showed that patients in both groups had equally increased ability to perform pain-free walking exercises and that treatment with EDTA did not result in any change in the patients' blood flow, red-cell viscosity, red-cell aggregation, or triglyceride and cholesterol levels. Diehm also concluded that the improvements in walking measurements in both groups were directly related to his success in convincing them of his strong interest in their well-being and his ability to motivate them to make an effort to perform greater activity.

In the second trial, R. Hopf, a cardiologist at the University of Frankfurt, tested chelation in patients with coronary heart disease. In this trial, 16 patients with angiographic evidence of coronary heart disease were randomized and divided into an EDTA-treated and an untreated group. Before treatment, the treated group averaged 2.1 significantly narrowed coronary arteries, while the untreated group averaged 2.6. Patients were infused with 500 ml of either the EDTA solution or dilute salt water (a placebo) at three-day intervals for a total of 20 infusions. On completion of the trial, patients in both groups said they felt better and performed weightlifting tests equally well. However, comparison of both groups before and after treatment, using angiography and other tests, indicated no improvement in blood flow through the patients' coronary arteries and a slight progression of their atherosclerosis. Hopf concluded that chelation had no effect on diseased coronary arteries.

Dubious Claims About the Safety of Chelation Therapy

Proponents also claim that chelation has been demonstrated to be safe. In *Bypassing Bypass*, Cranton declares that six million chelation treatments have been given safely over the last forty years. In his textbook, however, he warns of the seriousness of the possible side effects and advises that prospective patients be given a complete physical examination and be tested to rule out hypocalcemia, kidney impairment, allergic conditions (sensitivity to components of the EDTA infusion fluids), hypoglycemia, blood-clotting problems, congestive heart failure, liver impairment, and tuberculosis.

Other observers have reported cases of hypocalcemia leading to cardiac arrhythmias and tetany; kidney damage; decreased blood-clotting ability with abnormal bleeding; thrombophlebitis and embolism; hypoglycemia and insulin shock; severe vasculitis and autoimmune-related hemolytic anemia; dermatitis with pruritus and generalized eczema; and extensive clumping of platelets in the blood of some patients with atherosclerosis and other chronic diseases.

An important theoretical consideration should also be considered. The trace metal most dramatically lost as a result of EDTA chelation is zinc. French researchers have found that

24 hours after an infusion of EDTA, the urine of human subjects contained 15 times the normal amount of zinc. Without replacement, the loss of this much zinc over the months during which 30 to 40 treatments are delivered will increase the potential for severe impairment of immune function, precancerous cellular mutations, loss in selective permeability of cell membranes, and altered solubility of pancreatic insulin. Although proponent literature advises that supplemental zinc be administered to guard against zinc depletion, studies showing that this supplementation actually prevents depletion have not been published in the peer-reviewed scientific literature. . . .

The Phantom Study

In October 1989, chelation therapy was listed as one of the "Top Ten Health Frauds" in an article in *FDA Consumer*. The article reported that both the FDA [US Food and Drug Administration] and the American Heart Association have said that there is no scientific evidence that chelation therapy is effective against cardiovascular disease. Three issues later, a letter from a proponent complained that the listing was inappropriate because the FDA had approved the protocol of a clinical trial that was under way. The letter was followed by "an apology for the error," which stated that the editor had not been aware that chelation therapy had been approved for a study. The editor's note also quoted an FDA official who said that the study should "unequivocally answer at least several questions related to the utility of chelation therapy in . . . intermittent claudication."

The FDA should not have backed down because mere approval for a clinical trial is not proof that method works. Nevertheless, for several years, proponents continued to trumpet the *existence* of the study as evidence that their claims were justified. The study, however, has not been completed. According to proponents, a drug company that was involved in funding the study changed its mind, leaving them without the resources to complete it. Even if the study had been completed and had demonstrated benefit in patients with intermittent claudication, it would not have proven that chelation is safe or effective for anything else.

In 1992, a group of cardiovascular surgeons in Denmark published results of a double-blinded, randomized, placebo-controlled study of EDTA treatment for severe intermittent claudication. A total of 153 patients in two groups received 20 infusions of EDTA or a placebo for 5 to 9 weeks, in a clinical protocol duplicating the conditions used by Olszewer and Carter in 1990. The changes seen in pain-free and maximal walking distances were similar for the EDTA-treated and the placebo group, and there were no long-term therapeutic effects noted in 3-month and 6-month follow-ups. These investigators concluded that chelation was not effective against intermittent claudication.

The Consensus of Scientists and Medical Groups Is That Chelation Does Not Work

Chelation therapists state they have administered millions of EDTA treatments to hundreds of thousands of patients over the past 40 years. Protagonist publications contain their claims of numerous clinical successes and speculations couched in modern scientific terms, seeking to explain how chelation therapy could work. Since there is no evidence showing the treatment has modified the disease process, it is clear that the "benefits" being described are the result of the compassionate attention paid to the problems of the patient and to the encouragement given them to cope with their symptoms, and/or to changes in patients' lifestyle, the same ones recommended by scientific practitioners.

If chelation therapists practiced in a scientific manner, their publications would show an interest in obtaining objective proof that chelation could alter the progress of the atherosclerosis, that occluded blood vessels could be cleared, that plaque deposits could be reduced, and that hardened arteries could be "softened." Their data would include carefully documented case reports with long-term follow-up, comparisons of angiograms or ultrasound tests before and after chelation, and data from autopsies of former patients. But chelationists have published no such data. The few well-designed studies that have addressed the efficacy of chelation for atherosclerotic diseases have been carried out by "establishment" medical scientists. Without exception, these found no evidence that chelation worked.

Based on numerous reviews of the world's medical literature, these same conclusions have been reached by the FDA, the FTC [US Federal Trade Commission], National Institutes of Health, National Research Council, . . . American Medical Association, Centers for Disease Control and Prevention, American Heart Association, American College of Physicians, American Academy of Family Physicians, American Society for Clinical Pharmacology [and] Therapeutics, American College of Cardiology, and American Osteopathic Association.

Notwithstanding claims to the contrary, the chelation "establishment" is not being victimized by a prejudiced and arrogant medical orthodoxy but by its own unwillingness to mount a rigorous, placebo-controlled, double-blind clinical trial and stand by the results.

Periodical and Internet Sources Bibliography

The following articles have been selected to supplement the diverse views presented in this chapter.

Marissa Cevallos	"Meditation Instead of Morphine—Not So Fast," *Los Angeles Times*, April 7, 2011.
European Committee for Homeopathy	"Research Study Shows Effectiveness of Homeopathy in Insomnia," National Center for Homeopathy, September 13, 2010. http://nationalcenterforhomeopathy.org.
David H. Freedman	"Angry Responses to My Piece on Alternative Medicine," Making Sense of Medicine and Obesity, June 17, 2011. www.msomed.org.
David H. Freedman	"The Triumph of New-Age Medicine," *Atlantic*, July/August 2011.
Anne Harding	"In Pain? Try Meditation," CNN.com, April 5, 2011. www.cnn.com.
Rainer Lüdtke	"Is It the Homeopathic Case-Taking that Helps, or the Homeopathic Medicine?," *Homeopathy Research Institute Newsletter*, no. 12, Spring 2011, pp. 1–2.
Lionel R. Milgrom	"When Sorry Seems to Be the Hardest Word: CAM, Free Speech, and the British Legal System," *Homeopathy*, vol. 99, 2010.
Steven Novella	"Alt Med Apologetics at the *Atlantic*," *NeuroLogica Blog*, June 16, 2011. http://theness.com.
Steven Salzberg	"A 'Triumph' of Hype over Reality," *Atlantic*, June 16, 2011.
Carolyn Schatz	"Mindfulness Meditation Improves Connections in the Brain," *Harvard Health Blog*, April 8, 2011. www.health.harvard.edu.

OPPOSING
VIEWPOINTS®
SERIES

CHAPTER 2

Why Is Alternative Medicine Popular?

Chapter Preface

Talk show host and popular culture icon Oprah Winfrey has been taken to task by the medical and scientific establishment many times over the course of her more than two decades in the national spotlight. Many doctors bemoan the problems created by the public's belief in celebrity "health experts," charging that their so-called "cures" can often do more harm than good for public health, and that in some cases they can be downright dangerous. Because Winfrey has been shown time and time again to be far and above other celebrities in terms of her vast influence on public opinion, health advocates are particularly dismayed when she promotes what they believe to be dangerous, unscientific advice. Actress Jenny McCarthy, who cautions against childhood vaccines because she believes they cause autism, was a frequent guest on Winfrey's show. Further, the claims of Suzanne Somers, a staunch advocate of the controversial bioidentical hormone replacement therapy as well as other widely criticized alternative treatments, were given a significant boost by Winfrey when she wrote in *O, The Oprah Magazine*: "After one day on bioidentical estrogen, I felt the veil lift. . . . After three days, the sky was bluer, my brain was no longer fuzzy, my memory was sharper. I was literally singing and had a skip in my step."[1]

Winfrey's coverage of thyroid disease on her show, blog, and in her magazine has been lamented by patient advocates, doctors, and those who suffer from thyroid disease, which disproportionately affects women. In October 2007, Winfrey wrote that she had "first hyperthyroidism, which sped up my metabolism and left me unable to sleep for days. . . . Then hypothyroidism, which slowed down my metabolism and made me want to sleep all the time."[2] To cure herself of what she characterized as lack of "balance" in her thyroid gland and in her life, Winfrey gave herself a month off to rest and rejuvenate. In a later discussion about her thyroid disease on her television program, Winfrey told her audience that she had also taken thyroid medications during that time, but that she had since stopped taking them. For insight into thyroid disorder Winfrey consulted Dr. Christiane Northrup, who says on her website: "In many women thyroid dysfunction develops because of an energy blockage in the throat region, the result of a lifetime of 'swallowing' words one is aching to say."[3] *Newsweek* contributors Weston Kosova and Patricia Wingert remarked: "An interesting theory—but is there anyone who believes that what Oprah suffers from is an inability to express herself?"[4]

Kosova and Wingert go on to quote Dr. David Cooper, a professor of endocrinology at Johns Hopkins medical school who specializes in thyroid disorder: "Thyroid disease has nothing to do with women being downtrodden. She [Northrup] makes it sound like these women brought it on themselves." Mary Shomon, author of numerous books, blogs, and articles on thyroid disorder, concurs and declares: "Here's my wake-up call to women everywhere: Thyroid disease is NOT your fault. Thyroid disease results when heredity and genetics, autoimmunity, environmental exposures, viral infections, and hormonal shifts come together in a perfect storm to trigger a dysfunction. And while emotional and physical stress, as well as nutrition and lifestyle, can play a role in creating a climate receptive for—or fighting against—most diseases including thyroid conditions, these factors are only part of a larger, complicated puzzle."[5] Shomon continues: "I don't care if Oprah herself has embraced Dr. Northrup's theory. That is still no reason for any woman to believe that she is to blame, much less that blowing kisses to herself in the mirror and taking a hot bath before bed will resolve her hormonal imbalances, as Dr. Northrup suggested on the show."

The influence of celebrity endorsements on the popularity of alternative medicine is just one subject covered in this chapter of *Opposing Viewpoints: Alternative Medicine.* The viewpoints in this chapter address the cultural and political factors surrounding alternative medicine's popularity as well as the economic, psychological, and practical reasons behind the growing public interest in nontraditional treatments.

Notes

1. Oprah Winfrey, "To: Oprah Winfrey; Subject: Hormones," *O, The Oprah Magazine,* February 2009.
2. Oprah Winfrey, "Giving Myself a Month Off," *O, The Oprah Magazine,* October 2007.
3. Christiane Northrup, "Thyroid Disease," *Christiane Northrup, M.D.,* 2009. www.drnorthrup.com.
4. Weston Kosova and Patricia Wingert, "Live Your Best Life Ever!," *Newsweek,* May 29, 2009. www.thedailybeast.com.
5. Mary Shomon, "An Open Letter to Oprah's Viewers About Thyroid Disease: Your Thyroid Condition Is NOT Your Own Fault," About.com, October 16, 2007. http://thyroid.about.com.

| "Why is alternative medicine so popular in America? . . . Politics. While the Left and Right almost never agree, neither wants the government to mess with their medicine cabinet."

Politics and Culture Contribute to Alternative Medicine's Popularity

Rahul Parikh

Rahul Parikh is a San Francisco Bay area pediatrician, a contributor of articles on medical topics to a variety of publications, and is the author of the PopRx column on Salon.com. In the following viewpoint, Parikh explains that deep-seated characteristics of American identity such as opposition to authority and regulation make alternative medicine appealing to Americans. He outlines how the growing popularity of alternative medicine was supported by powerful legislators from both political parties who fought to loosen US Food and Drug Administration regulation of dietary supplements and fund the National Center for Complementary and Alternative Medicine (NCCAM). Parikh illustrates how current health challenges such as managing chronic

Rahul Parikh, "Why Does Your Doctor Hate Alternative Medicine?," Salon.com, May 2, 2011. Copyright © 2011 by Salon.com. All rights reserved. Reproduced by permission.

diseases like cancer and diabetes lead consumers to seek out cures that traditional medicine has not yet discovered. Parikh maintains that doctors do not object to alternative medicine itself but rather to the lack of government oversight and regulation of dietary supplements and other natural remedies. Parikh suggests that consumers should be wary of alternative treatments and should seek out reputable sources of information to become better educated about viable options for care.

As you read, consider the following questions:

1. What US senator was instrumental in the establishment of the National Center for Complementary and Alternative Medicine, according to Parikh?

2. How many complaints about adverse events caused by ephedra were received by MetaboLife, according to the viewpoint?

3. What danger does St. John's wort present to patients with HIV/AIDS, according to Parikh?

On his popular TV show last week [April 26, 2011], Dr. Mehmet Oz ran a segment titled "Why Your Doctor Is Afraid of Alternative [Health]." The show pitted Oz (who has found himself under fire for dubious doctoring) against Dr. Steve Novella, a Yale neurologist and blogger who is skeptical of alt-med [alternative medicine] treatments.

Who won? You can watch the videos for yourself. But ultimately, it doesn't matter, because in the real world—i.e., drugstore aisles across America—the business of alternative and complementary medicine is booming. Studies show that 1 in 3 Americans have tried alternative therapies, generating close to $50 billion in sales for the industry. So let's zero in on a different question: Why is alternative medicine so popular in America?

Politics and National Identities Have a Major Impact on Alternative Medicine

The reasons, of course, are many. But here's one unexpected answer: Politics. While the Left and Right almost never agree, neither wants the government to mess with their medicine cabinet. The Left has that anti-authority streak that bristles at the medical establishment, while the Right has a visceral opposition to any government regulation—in this case, the Food and Drug Administration [FDA]. In fact, the history of the modern alternative medical movement started in the halls of Congress back in the early 1990s. That's when Democratic Sen. Tom Harkin, having cured his allergies using bee pollen, became an alt-med convert. Harkin controlled the purse strings of the National Institutes of Health. He took $2 million of its then $11 billion budget and, to the dismay of many scientists, established the National Center for Complementary and Alternative Medicine (NCCAM). Later in the decade, Harkin's Republican colleague, Sen. Orrin Hatch of Utah, joined the fight. Like Harkin, Hatch believed that bee pollen had cured his allergies. In an effort to choke off the FDA's ability to regulate dietary supplements, the two wrote the Dietary Supplement Health and Education Act in 1994. The law passed unanimously, shielding the supplement industry from anything other than voluntary regulation. With the FDA able to intervene only after the drug has been made available to the public (as opposed to its typical, rigorous product testing before a drug hits shelves everywhere), a business began to explode. (It's worth noting that many alternative medicine and dietary supplement companies are based in Hatch's home state of Utah.)

But there are qualities in the American psyche that also favor alternative remedies. First, there's our natural inclination to keep fighting no matter the odds (other cultures are certainly more fatalistic). Our can-do attitude fuels a desire to explore any and all frontiers—be it the West, space or the cutting edge of medicine. Second, science, including medical science, just isn't what it used to be. Paul Starr, in his Pulitzer Prize–winning book *The Social Transformation of American Medicine*, recalls that the post–World War II decades "gave science unprecedented recognition as a national asset . . . the research effort that produced radar, the atom bomb and penicillin persuaded even the skeptical that science was vital to national security."

But as the Berlin Wall fell, our collective psyche lost that sense of scientific superiority, which coincided with a growing recognition that medicine had limits, and that we were spending a lot of money on health care with ever-diminishing returns. Medicine and doctors' reputations declined as we moved from curing acute illness—like infections with antibiotics and vaccines—to battling the tyranny of the chronic: heart disease, diabetes, cancer and others. These are complicated diseases and some, like chronic fatigue syndrome, are poorly understood. There's nothing in medicine that can cure most of these ailments, and their treatments usually mean lifelong doses of medications, tests and hospitalizations, all of which have side effects. Skepticism crept in, and with it, room for alternative views. Cancer, where chemotherapy can kill you just as readily as the disease itself, is ripe with alternative medical therapies, from homeopathy to herbal medicine to faith healing.

Doctors Object to a Lack of Oversight and Regulation

All that aside, I don't think Mehmet Oz's assertion—that doctors are afraid of alternative medicine—is fair or correct. (For that matter, I don't think similar assertions made by other altmed media mavens like Deepak Chopra are, either.) It sets up the stereotypical "us versus them" conflict that TV producers love, but the real world is far more nuanced. Out here, it's more accurate to say most doctors have a love-hate relation-

Popular Alternative Medicine Proponents Promote Pseudoscience

[Dr. Andrew] Weil "frames" his version of "integrative medicine" not . . . as "integrating" quackery with science but rather as aiming to:

1. Restore the focus of medical teaching, research, and practice on health and healing;

2. Develop "whole person" medicine, in which the mental, emotional and spiritual dimensions of human beings are included in diagnosis and treatment, along with the physical body;

3. Take all aspects of diet and lifestyle into account in assessing health and the root causes of disease;

4. Protect and emphasize the practitioner/patient relationship as central to the healing process;

5. Emphasize disease prevention and health promotion.

These are all noble ideas, but none of them requires integrating pseudoscience and belief-based medicine with SBM [science-based medicine]. . . .

There's a reason why promoters of unscientific medicine . . . are focusing so heavily on medical education and setting up "integrative medicine" programs at academic medical centers and bolstering its consortium of CAM [complementary and alternative medicine]-friendly academic medical centers. They're playing for the long term; there's no doubt about that. . . . The infrastructure is rapidly being built to subvert science in the bastions of academia and replace it with quackademic medicine.

David Gorski,
"Blatant Pro-Alternative Medicine Propaganda
in The Atlantic," *Science-Based Medicine, June 20, 2011.*
www.sciencebasedmedicine.org.

ship with alternative medicine. We want to know—and care about—what health tricks people are trying off the prescription pad. Our frustration comes in because we have very little idea whether or not these medicines are safe and effective. That's because, as I mentioned earlier, the alt-med business is accountable to nobody. That's unlike conventional pharmaceuticals, which go through rigorous testing before they're approved for sale and are subject to close oversight once they're on the shelves of pharmacies.

As doctors, we rely on the FDA to help us determine whether a drug is safe and effective. If it's safe but not effective, you can take all you want because it's not going to hurt you. On the other hand, if it's unsafe and ineffective, it could kill you. For most of the stuff packed into alternative pill bottles, we have no idea which is a blessing and which is a curse.

Take the once popular, now banned alt-med ephedra. Athletes and body builders gravitated to it as a performance enhancer. Then people started getting sick. One company that made ephedra, MetaboLife, received 13,000 complaints of adverse events. When the FDA dug deeper into the ephedra problem in 1997, it ran into the formidable duo of Sens. Harkin and Hatch, who—along with millions of dollars from the supplement industry—stopped the agency faster than a speeding bullet. But that didn't stop doctors from looking more closely. In 2000, the *New England Journal of Medicine* published a paper linking cases of sudden death to ephedra. Still, no ban. Then in 2001 and 2003, two professional athletes, Korey Stringer of the Minnesota Vikings and Steve Bechler of the Baltimore Orioles, died due to ephedra toxicity. Their deaths were the Kryptonite the FDA needed to push for and finally ban the drug in 2004.

The problems with alternative medicines can also be more subtle than death, and therefore, harder to find. Consider one popular alt-med remedy for depression—St. John's wort. While it's thought to help mild to moderate depression, it can harm patients with HIV/AIDS by lowering levels of their vital anti-viral drugs. We didn't know this until scientists, and not the dietary supplement industry, researched it. And you still won't see any warnings about it on the bottle's label. Had the FDA done its due diligence on St. John's wort, it would have made that discovery and put it in the drug information available to health professionals and HIV patients everywhere.

Consumers Should Be Cautious and Educate Themselves

So what's an empowered, motivated patient to do when standing in front of the herb and supplement aisle at Whole Foods? My only advice is something a friend and mentor of mine once told me. "Be open-minded, but not so much that your brains fall out." For what it's worth, the NCCAM website can provide some education about various alt-med remedies. On the other hand, it's worth noting 2009 reports that despite having spent $2.5 billion in taxpayer dollars looking into alternative therapies, the government hasn't found much that works.

Despite that news, none of this is going away anytime soon. First, because celebri-docs like Mehmet Oz (along with Deepak Chopra, Mark Hyman, Christiane Northrup and others) are out there speaking to millions with their endorsements of alt-med remedies. Then there are the celebrities who aren't doctors, like Suzanne Somers and Jenny McCarthy, attesting to their own stories. "I have my science. His name is Evan," McCarthy is fond of saying (referring to her son).

An ironic twist in all this is that mainstream doctors, who once shunned colleagues pushing alternative remedies, now see an opportunity to make money right alongside them. That's why many well-respected academic centers—from Harvard to UCSF [University of California, San Francisco]—now have centers for alternative medicine. "If hospitals don't get involved in these kinds of programs, they will lose patients because patients will go elsewhere," said one former health care executive.

Perhaps the wisest insight in this debate comes not from a health expert but a jester, Australian comedian Tim Minchin. "You know what they call alternative medicine that's been proved to work? Medicine."

> *"[Acupuncture] . . . is used at a low level by a small to moderate proportion of the population for conditions that are either mild, self-limiting, or without a definitive conventional treatment, and it is rarely used in lieu of conventional medical care."*

The Popularity of Alternative Medicine Is Exaggerated

Brennen McKenzie

Brennen McKenzie is a licensed veterinarian, contributor of articles on medicine and science to a variety of publications, and the author of the SkeptVet Blog. In the following viewpoint, McKenzie uses statistics and research to illustrate that there is no reliable evidence to support the widespread belief that acupuncture is widely used and growing in popularity. The author cites various studies and statistics from around the world that indicate that while there are variations in culture, nationality, access to health care, and overall percentage of use, acupuncture is not utilized with nearly the frequency or by nearly as many people as is commonly reported. Even in areas of the world such as

China and Taiwan, where acupuncture-use rates would be expected to be very high, McKenzie asserts that the statistics show that the percentages are modest at best.

As you read, consider the following questions:

1. What was the only form of medical therapy classified as alternative that was used by more than 10 percent of Americans surveyed in the Centers for Disease Control and Prevention's 2007 National Health Interview Survey (NHIS), according to McKenzie?

2. According to the 2007 NHIS cited by McKenzie, for what type of health problem did the vast majority of Americans seek acupuncture treatment?

3. What percentage of national health insurance beneficiaries in Taiwan used acupuncture, according to a 2007 study cited by McKenzie?

One argument that often comes up when skeptics and proponents of so-called complementary and alternative medicine (CAM) debate is the question of the popularity of various CAM practices. Advocates of CAM often claim these practices are widely used and growing rapidly in popularity. Obviously, CAM proponents have an interest in characterizing their practices as widely accepted and utilized. Even though the popularity of an idea is not a reliable indication of whether or not it is true, most people are inclined to accept that if a lot of people believe in something there must be at least some truth to it. The evidence against this idea is overwhelming, but it is a deeply intuitive, intransigent notion that can only rarely be dislodged.

It might therefore be useful to get some idea of whether or not the claims of great popularity for CAM treatments are true. If they are not, fruitless debates about the probative value of such popularity could potentially be avoided, and it might be possible to diminish the allure associated with the belief that "everybody's doing it."

It is difficult to find good-quality, objective data on the popularity of particular CAM interventions, and many of the surveys that have been done are potentially misleading. For example, the 2007 CDC [Centers for Disease Control and Prevention] National Health Interview Survey (NHIS) is widely cited as showing that about 30% of Americans use CAM therapies. A careful look at the details of this survey, however, shows that many of the supposed CAM therapies are really relaxation or exercise practices, such as massage and yoga, not medical therapies. Chiropractic is the only medical therapy generally classified as alternative that was used by more than 10% of people in the survey. And that was primarily for idiopathic lower-back pain, an indication for which it is generally accepted, even by skeptics such as myself, as having some demonstrated benefit, about equal to standard medical interventions. These usage numbers haven't changed in decades, which belies the notion that CAM is growing in popularity. Similarly, much was made by the media of a recent CDC survey that supposedly showed widespread use of CAM therapies in hospice care facilities. A close analysis of this survey, also shows that most of the therapies listed are not truly alternative medical interventions and that fewer than half the facilities surveyed offered true CAM therapies, and fewer than 10% of patients in those facilities actually employed the CAM practices offered.

Studies of Acupuncture Use Show That Utilization Is Generally Low

I thought it might be useful to look at some of the data concerning the popularity of acupuncture, since it is probably the most widely used and accepted CAM therapy after chiropractic, and there have been a few interesting studies in this area.

There are certainly no comprehensive, high-quality data concerning how many people use acupuncture, for what indications, and with what sort of beliefs in its underlying theory or effectiveness. My purpose is not to make a definitive statement about how popular acupuncture is but simply to take a small step beyond vague impressions and unsupported claims about the popularity of this intervention and look at what research there is and what insight, if any, these numbers might give us.

The 2007 NHIS data indicated 6.5% of Americans had reported ever using acupuncture. Of these, 22% had seen an acupuncturist in the last 12 months. 25% of those who had tried acupuncture had done so once, and 70% had seen an acupuncturist fewer than 5 times. The vast majority of those who had seen an acupuncturist had done so for some kind of pain, primarily arthritis and other orthopedic pain, headaches, or fibromyalgia. About 40% of the people who reported using acupuncture for a specific condition specifically reported *not* using conventional therapies for that condition, while 20–40% reported using some kind of conventional medical therapy for the same condition.

It is often argued that lack of interest in utilizing acupuncture is driven more by cultural prejudice or belief systems than by concerns about the evidence for its efficacy. There is likely some truth to the fact that people from different cultures prefer familiar styles of medical treatment, though of course this says nothing about what is actually safe or effective. And part of the appeal of acupuncture in the West is likely its exotic, "foreign" associations.

Some surveys of acupuncture use have looked at whether different ethnic groups in the West have differences in their utilization of acupuncture. Interestingly, one study from Canada found that while white and Chinese Canadians differed in their use of some CAM modalities, their overall use of CAM was the same, and their use of acupuncture specifically was about the same: roughly 8%. (Therapies included in

[the] definition of CAM in [H.] Quan et al. 2008: Herbal remedies, massage therapy, chiropractic, acupuncture, amino acids, naturopathy, homeopathy, reiki, ayurvedic medicine, biofeedback, hypnosis.)

In contrast, a survey of Chinese Americans in a mental health services program found about 25% used acupuncture, and that this use was more prevalent among "less acculturated" individuals. This, of course, is a group not at all representative of the general population, so the relevance of this to overall acupuncture use among Chinese Americans and Americans of other ethnicities is not clear. Other studies have shown significant but complex relationships between ethnicity, education, and other variables and the likelihood of acupuncture use.

It seems reasonable that cultural traditions play some role in the acceptance or rejection of acupuncture as a medical therapy, but the current data do not support that cultural affiliation alone is the most important variable, and the reasons people use acupuncture seem quite consistent regardless of ethnicity or nationality. In any case, studies of populations in North America do not show anything approaching a majority of the population regularly using acupuncture as a medical therapy. Numbers vary from less than 10% to as high as 50% in some populations, but most tend to be in the lower end of that range. Since acupuncture as it is currently understood and practiced in Europe and North America originated in China and has been employed there and in other Asian countries for a lot longer than it has been used in the West (though not nearly as long as is usually claimed), it makes sense that it would be far more widely used in that part of the world if it is truly as popular a therapy as its proponents claim.

One 2007 study in Taiwan found about 11% of beneficiaries of national health insurance had used acupuncture in a given year. Interestingly, while the survey found that overall use of traditional Chinese medicine (TCM) therapies was much higher than this (primarily due to use of herbal remedies), the use of TCM was still far behind the use of so-called "Western" medicine. TCM clinic visits accounted for only 9% of outpatient visits reimbursed under the national health insurance. This is similar to another study which found Chinese medicine (of all covered types) accounted for only 5% of the reimbursed care under the national health insurance system. The same study indicated that "Western" medicine was utilized more than Chinese medicine, especially among children, the elderly, and those with severe disease (consistent with the pattern of CAM use in the U.S., which is generally for self-limiting or chronic disease).

Yet another study in Taiwan specifically investigated acupuncture use and found about 6.2% of people covered by national health insurance utilized acupuncture in a given year, and over the seven years surveyed about 25% of covered individuals had received acupuncture treatment. As in the U.S., the vast majority of the acupuncture treatment sought was for musculoskeletal conditions or injuries (88%). And a recently published series of surveys conducted in Japan found that about 5–7% of respondents used acupuncture in a given year, and that over a lifetime between 20–27% of respondents had at some time tried acupuncture. More than 80% of the use of acupuncture was for musculoskeletal complaints. About half of those who had used acupuncture indicated they would use it again, and about 37% indicated they would not.

The Bottom Line Is That Acupuncture Does Not Appear to Be Very Popular

So what does all of this mean? Well, probably not very much. Of course, differences in health care systems, insurance systems, study methods, and many other factors that are difficult to identify and assess make direct comparisons between the use of specific CAM interventions in different countries very unreliable. I don't believe the quality of the data generally allow very confident statements about the popularity of acupuncture or other specific CAM methods. However, proponents of acupuncture and CAM generally often make such statements, trying to convey the impression that their approaches are growing rapidly in popularity and only perverse, closed-minded curmudgeons still resist them. The little evidence we have certainly does not support such claims.

In the case of acupuncture, for example, the data show relatively low levels of utilization even in those countries generally regarded as having long historical traditions of using acupuncture. Informal investigations have suggested that acupuncture and other CAM practices associated with China may not be as popular even in their native land as proponents in North America claim, and the formal studies I have discussed here seem to support that impression.

A large majority of people who seek acupuncture therapy, regardless of ethnicity or nationality, do so for treatment of musculoskeletal conditions and pain. There is good evidence that the therapeutic ritual of acupuncture has some symptomatic benefit for such indications. This is almost certainly a nonspecific treatment effect (aka "placebo"). It does not seem to matter where needles are inserted or if they are inserted at all, and acupuncture therapy does not appear to measurably affect the course of any actual disease.

The research data on acupuncture utilization suggests that from about 5–25% of people, regardless of nationality or ethnicity, will at some time try acupuncture, mostly for some kind of musculoskeletal pain. Conventional therapies are often used along with acupuncture, and they are far more popular overall, especially for serious or acute conditions. So the little research there is suggests that acupuncture occupies a niche common to many CAM therapies. It is used at a low level by a small to moderate proportion of the population for conditions that are either mild, self-limiting, or without a definitive conventional treatment, and it is rarely used in lieu of conventional medical care. This is hardly a mounting wave of enthusiasm for acupuncture itself, much less the mystical theories and postmodern cognitive relativism often associated with it.

So when proponents of acupuncture say it must work because it has been widely used for thousands of years in Asia and is growing rapidly in popularity in the West, rebutting the *arsumentum ad populum* [something believed to be true because it is popular] and *argumentum ad antiquitatem* [something believed to be true because it is tradition or common] fallacies may not be the skeptic's only option. It may be worthwhile, and simpler, just to point out that acupuncture is neither as old nor as popular as is commonly supposed.

"Not one modality has all the answers. There [are] some aspects we understand rigorously and scientifically, and some we don't. . . . Basically it comes down to if you try one and it doesn't work, you try to find an answer on the other side."

The Prevalence of Complementary Treatments Reflects Frustration with Traditional Medicine

Lauren Cox

Lauren Cox is a reporter for the ABC News Medical Unit. In the following viewpoint, she explores the variety of reasons—ranging from low cost to distrust of the medical establishment—why more and more individual Americans and medical providers are utilizing alternative medicine either in addition to or in place of traditional medicine. Cox asserts that despite the fact that the American Medical Association has failed to endorse alternative treatments, their use for the treatment of chronic illnesses con-

Lauren Cox, "Why Do We Spend $34 Billion in Alternative Medicine?," ABCNews.com, July 31, 2009. www.abcnews.go.com. Copyright © 2009 by ABCNews.com. All rights reserved. Reproduced by permission.

tinues to grow, as does the number of naturopathic doctors. Cox reports that two-thirds of Americans' out-of-pocket expenditures on alternative medicine were for self-prescribed dietary supplements and for classes such as yoga. Furthermore, naturopathic practitioners have expressed concern over the unsupervised use of supplements that can, they warn, be dangerous if taken inappropriately. Cox relates that in states where naturopathic doctors are licensed, treatment is coordinated between naturopathic and traditional doctors, and it is cooperative and integrative rather than oppositional.

As you read, consider the following questions:

1. What percentage of Americans' 2007 out-of-pocket health care expenses went to alternative therapies, according to the viewpoint?

2. How many states, according to Cox, recognize naturopathic doctors as licensed medical providers?

3. What alternative modalities does the Association of Accredited Naturopathic Medical Colleges state are combined in naturopathy, according to the viewpoint?

Chances are that one out of every three people you see in the grocery store, on the street or at work have tried alternative medicine, and they're spending quite a bit for it.

The National Institutes of Health (NIH) announced Thursday that Americans spent $34 billion on complementary and alternative medicine in 2007. The study queried more than 70,000 people across the country about 36 various forms of alternative treatments.

But researchers say they still don't know exactly why people are turning to these therapies.

"Since this was a point of time survey, we weren't necessarily asking people about why or how they made their deci-

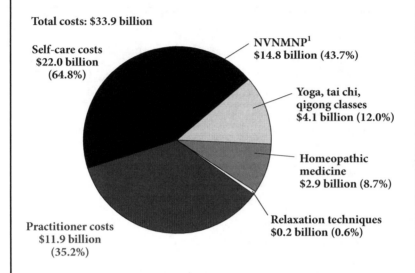

Out-of-Pocket Costs of Alternative Medicine Among US Adults

Total costs: $33.9 billion

Self-care costs
$22.0 billion
(64.8%)

NVNMNP[1]
$14.8 billion (43.7%)

Yoga, tai chi,
qigong classes
$4.1 billion (12.0%)

Homeopathic
medicine
$2.9 billion (8.7%)

Relaxation techniques
$0.2 billion (0.6%)

Practitioner costs
$11.9 billion
(35.2%)

[1] Nonvitamin, nonmineral, natural products.
NOTES: Percentages refer to the total out-of-pocket costs in 2007. Totaling individual self-care cost percentages is affected by rounding. Estimates are based on household interviews of a sample of the civilian, noninstitutionalized population.
DATA SOURCE: CDC/NCHS, National Health Interview Survey, 2007.

TAKEN FROM: Richard L. Nahin, Patricia M. Barnes, Barbara J. Stussman, and Barbara Bloom, "Costs of Complementary and Alternative Medicine (CAM) and Frequency of Visits to CAM Practitioners: United States 2007," National Health Statistics Reports, no. 18, US Department of Health and Human Services, July 30, 2009.

sion," said Richard Nahin, an author of the study released by the NIH and the National Center for Complementary and Alternative Medicine (NCCAM).

The $34 billion spent on complementary and alternative medicine pales in comparison to the $2.2 trillion spent on health care annually, but alternative therapies accounted for up to 10 percent of out-of-pocket health costs.

Barriers Between Traditional and Alternative Medicine May Be Breaking Down

Yet at the same time as Americans are embracing alternative medicine, the American Medical Association's (AMA's) policy on the matter far from endorses the treatments.

"There is little evidence to confirm the safety or efficacy of most alternative therapies," the AMA policy states. "Much of the information currently known about these therapies makes it clear that many have not been shown to be efficacious. Well-designed, stringently controlled research should be done to evaluate the efficacy of alternative therapies."

Without an explanation for exactly why an estimated 38 percent of the population in the United States has expanded their health spending beyond "Western medicine" doctors, NCCAM is simply trying to analyze where the money goes so the center may propose research to test whether it is safe or effective.

Anecdotally, the reasons why people choose alternative therapies range from the relatively cheap cost, the affinity for plant products and a mistrust of the medical establishment.

But an emergency room physician in Mesa, Ariz., who has recently turned to naturopathic care for his family, believes much of it has to do with chronic illness.

"At least in my world in allopathic medicine [a practice sometimes called Western medicine], we do much better with acute care than we do with chronic care," said Dr. Thomas Kupka. "I think for Americans as a whole, more and more of our health care is shifting into the chronic illnesses."

Kupka doesn't see alternative therapies as a replacement to Western medicine for chronic illnesses such as diabetes, hypertension or cancer. However, he did turn to a naturopathic doctor when oncologists said they had done all they could do for his cancer-stricken father.

Why People May Choose Alternative Therapies

"It's just my perspective that not one modality has all the answers. There [are] some aspects we understand rigorously and scientifically, and some we don't," said Kupka. "Basically it comes down to if you try one and it doesn't work, you try to find an answer on the other side."

Kupka said his father continues to see his oncologist but that he has improved since he started receiving care from a naturopathic doctor, or N.D.

"They gave him six weeks to live 15 weeks ago. His blood work all looks better than when they sent him home," said Kupka.

According to the NCCAM study, only one-third of the out-of-pocket costs that adults spend on alternative complementary medicine went to practitioners such as naturopaths. The other two-thirds went to "self-care" purchases of alternative medicine products, which include classes such as yoga and nonvitamin, nonmineral, natural products such as fish oil, glucosamine and echinacea.

Despite the widespread acceptance of alternative medicine in recent years, some naturopaths say they are worried about self-care purchases of supplements.

"The use of them is very complex. There is a lot of science that goes into choosing the right one," said Marnie Loomis, N.D., a director of professional formation at the National College of Natural Medicine in Portland, Ore.

"There are so many people out there thinking that natural equals safe, and that's not true," Loomis said.

Naturopathic doctors are recognized as licensed health care providers in 15 states, up from just a handful a few years ago.

The Association of Accredited Naturopathic Medical Colleges defines naturopathy as a do-no-harm holistic approach to medicine that "combines many methodologies, such as acupuncture, massage, chiropractic adjustment, homeopathy and herbal cures, along with sensible concepts such as good nutrition, exercise and relaxation techniques."

Loomis said in states where [naturopaths] are licensed, patients' care is almost uniformly coordinated with a mainstream doctor. But, her patients consistently say their dissatisfaction with their current doctor was the reason they chose to come to her.

Naturopaths Are Growing in Popularity

"From my personal experience in my practice, the phrase I heard most often was 'this is what I thought a doctor's office should look like,'" said Loomis.

"The visits are long, we talk about their entire health history as well as their lifestyle, what food they're eating, what are their exercise habits," she said. "Of the diseases out there—cancer, diabetes, obesity—they [patients] keep hearing that lifestyle is part of it, but they don't know how to do it. It is a learned skill."

Loomis said about two-thirds of her patients say extra attention to lifestyle was what motivated them to try her office. Anecdotally, some people who have lost their health insurance come to Loomis for a cheaper alternative.

But one-third comes out of frustration with their current treatment plans. Paul Mittman, N.D., president of Southwest College of Naturopathic Medicine and Health Sciences in Tempe, Ariz., said he's heard the occasional bristling against mainstream medicine.

"There are some people who come in with a mistrust of medicine, and it's often ironic because they expect to have a sympathetic ear, then I'll tell them, 'I think you need to go ahead and have that surgery,'" said Mittman, who noted four medical doctors work alongside naturopaths at his institution.

"That's one of the myths that persist, that it has to be oppositional," he said. "Integrating health care, integrating naturopathic medicine into patients' care is really the best way to practice."

"Many doctors say they're troubled by stars who cross the line from sharing their stories to championing questionable or even dangerous medical advice."

Celebrities Influence Public Interest in Alternative Treatments That Can Be Detrimental

Liz Szabo

Liz Szabo is a medical reporter for USA Today. *She specializes in articles on cancer, children's health, parenting, and environmental health. In the following viewpoint, Szabo examines some of the dangers presented by public acceptance of celebrity endorsements of unproven and potentially hazardous alternative health remedies. Szabo explains that celebrities can have a positive impact on public health by raising awareness about illnesses and preventive medical testing, as former first lady Betty Ford did when her public disclosure of her struggle with breast cancer and mastectomy prompted more women to get mammograms. Unfortunately, Szabo relates, when celebrities promote dangerous misinformation, as she explains actress Jenny McCarthy did when she launched a very public campaign citing a since disproven link between childhood vaccines and autism, the negative impact on public health can be profound. Doctors, she notes, find it very difficult to undo the damage done by celebrity health misinformation. The Internet, Szabo indicates, exacerbates the problem by providing a forum that offers false legitimacy to nonexpert medical information and anecdotal experiences.*

As you read, consider the following questions:

1. What did actor Tom Cruise dismiss as "pseudoscience" during a 2005 interview on *Today*, according to the viewpoint?

2. According to the viewpoint, what percentage of adults said that actress Jenny McCarthy's claims about vaccines have increased the likelihood that they will question vaccine safety?

3. What percentage of people indicated that they trust their doctors "a lot," and rated them higher than such sources of medical information as family, friends, the government, or the Internet, according to a 2007 study cited in the viewpoint?

When first lady Betty Ford announced that she had had a mastectomy in 1974, patient advocates say, it was groundbreaking. Breast-cancer survivors at the time were often afraid to mention their treatment, even to friends.

Today, many people in the public eye, particularly celebrities, feel comfortable sharing their medical problems.

Brooke Shields has acknowledged her postpartum depression. Michael J. Fox has written about his struggle with Parkinson's disease. Elizabeth Taylor updated fans about her heart surgery through Twitter.

Interest in Celebrities' Health Problems Is Understandable but Can Be Dangerous

Doctors say they can understand why patients sympathize with celebrities and closely follow their battles with serious illnesses.

"It helps people to realize that health problems they have affect even celebrities," says pediatrician Aaron Carroll, director of Indiana University's Center for Health Policy and Professionalism Research. "Knowing that a rich and famous person can have the same problem as you or me makes it seem more fair, maybe.

"It also can make it easier to talk about your own problem, because a celebrity has the same issue."

Yet celebrities—who can command huge audiences and sell thousands of books—have a special responsibility to get their facts right, says Bradford Hesse, who studies health communication at the National Cancer Institute [NCI]. Many doctors say they're troubled by stars who cross the line from sharing their stories to championing questionable or even dangerous medical advice.

- Tom Cruise in 2005 began a spat with Shields and drew criticism from mental health professionals when he railed against antidepressants and Ritalin on the *Today* show, dismissing psychiatry as a "pseudoscience."

- Actress Jenny McCarthy, who has an autistic son, has written several books linking autism with childhood vaccinations, even though a host of scientific studies show that vaccines are safe and not the cause of increasing autism rates.

- Actress Suzanne Somers—already well-known for her diet books and ThighMaster products—in October [2009] released her 18th book, *Knockout*, which experts describe as a catalogue of unproven or long-debunked alternative cancer "cures."

Reeducating Americans Who Are Misled by Celebrities

Doctors and public health groups say they struggle over the best way to respond to celebrity claims.

At Every Child By Two, an immunization campaign co-founded by former first lady Rosalynn Carter, board members were initially inclined to ignore celebrities who question vaccine safety, says executive director Amy Pisani. Now, the group spends 80% of its time explaining why vaccines are still critical.

"We were poised to start working in Africa," Pisani says. "But we were forced to pull back just to reeducate people here in the United States."

For good or bad, research shows that stars exert powerful influence not just on popular opinion, but on public health.

- Vaccines. A *USA Today*/Gallup poll of 1,017 adults found that more than half were aware of McCarthy's warnings about childhood shots. More than 40% of adults familiar with her message—23% of all adults surveyed—say McCarthy's claims have made them more likely to question vaccine safety. The Nov. 20–22 poll had a margin of error of plus or minus 4 percentage points.

- Colorectal cancer screening. The number of colonoscopies rose 20% in the year after TV news anchor Katie Couric, who lost her husband to the disease, had an on-air screening in 2001, according to a study in the *Archives of Internal Medicine*.

- HIV screening. The number of people being tested for HIV increased after [professional basketball player] Magic Johnson revealed in 1991 that he had tested positive for the virus, according to a study in New York State.

- Breast cancer screening. Diagnoses rose slightly in the year after Ford's mastectomy, possibly because more women were motivated to get mammograms, says the American Cancer Society's Otis Brawley.

- Breast cancer surgery. Nancy Reagan's mastectomy in 1987 may have influenced patients' choice of treatment. The number of women getting lumpectomies, instead of more extensive mastectomies, declined 25% in the months after Reagan's surgery, according to a study in the *Journal of the American Medical Association*.

Celebrities have the power to do tremendous good, Hesse says. Lance Armstrong, who survived testicular cancer, has advocated for funding and policy changes to help cancer patients and has raised more than $325 million through his foundation.

"People like Katie Couric and Lance Armstrong can do a lot to teach people that it is important to talk to their doctors about screening for cancer," Hesse says. "Some would say they have done more for the cause of public awareness for cancer than most scientists."

Yet celebrities also can spread misinformation much faster than the average person with a wacky theory, Hesse says.

Correcting that misinformation—even with a mountain of evidence—can be a challenge, says Paul Offit, chief of infectious diseases at Children's Hospital of Philadelphia. "It's much easier to scare people than to unscare them," Offit says.

By swaying parents to delay or reject childhood vaccines, celebrities could undermine efforts to protect newborns and other vulnerable children from devastating diseases, says pediatrician Martin Myers, executive director of the National Network for Immunization Information.

"I worry about these celebrities who confuse people," Myers says. "I don't think they know how much damage they can cause."

Celebrities' Medical Advice Can Be a Public Health Hazard

Celebrity medical advice can be hazardous. Their messages have led some doctors and patients to make inappropriate health decisions, at times increasing risks for patients and driving up health care costs. Their advocacy, while informative and inspiring, often oversimplifies complex medical issues. Finally, the first-class advantages most celebrities enjoy can create false hope for their economy-class public.

Rahul Parikh, "Doc Hollywood," Slate,
December 9, 2009. www.slate.com.

"The University of Google"

Some psychologists say that celebrity activists are part of a larger trend, in which survivors of serious illness feel less of a stigma about speaking out and find it therapeutic to help others in a similar situation.

"Giving to other people has a profound way of rewarding us," says the NCI's Julia Rowland. "It's a way to make meaning out of a situation. . . . You tell other people how to cope, and it helps you cope, too."

Others note that celebrities give voice to frustrations shared by many Americans.

"If someone has a heartfelt belief that something ought to be on the radar screen of America, they ought to put it out there, because believe me, other people are saying it anyway," says Mehmet Oz, a heart surgeon and host of *The Dr. Oz Show*. "I'd rather have it come up publicly and have Larry King have a debate about it."

Studies show that doctors still have great influence. About 68% of people trust their doctors "a lot," according to a 2007 survey by the NCI, giving them higher ratings than any other source, such as family, friends, the government, the Internet or other media.

In a televised debate, however, Oz says that a telegenic actor has a natural advantage over bespectacled scientists, however well-meaning and knowledgeable.

Yet personal testimonies, however compelling, also can be misleading, says Offit, who helped develop a vaccine against a deadly infection called rotavirus.

As a patient or parent, "you know about your particular situation, but that doesn't make you an expert in the field," Offit says. "It's part of our culture now. We believe we can be experts by simply looking on the Internet."

In her book *Mother Warriors*, McCarthy, who declined to be interviewed for this [viewpoint], says she learned about autism from "the university of Google."

Explaining complex science—especially in the few minutes allotted on a TV program—is challenging, Carroll says. Audiences sympathize with McCarthy, who says she doesn't need science because she observes her son, Evan, every day. "At home," she writes, "Evan is my science."

"How can you argue with that?" Carroll asks. "It's her child. It's her body. They win."

That's why Pisani says she urges parents to speak out about the need for vaccines. Actress Amanda Peet now works with vaccine groups, encouraging parents to get their medical advice from doctors, rather than celebrities like herself.

Oz says doctors must do a better job of putting a human face on medical questions while showing that they take people's concerns seriously.

"Ten percent of people are going to believe in Suzanne Somers anyway," Oz says. "What I don't want is to have 50% more people go there."

Periodical and Internet Sources Bibliography

The following articles have been selected to supplement the diverse views presented in this chapter.

Tom Blackwell	"Ontario's Move Toward Alternative Medicine Draws Sharp Criticism," *National Post*, September 30, 2011.
Michelle Brandt	"Americans' Use of Complementary Medicine on the Rise," *Scope*, February 1, 2011. http://scopeblog.stanford.edu.
Bruce Kennedy	"As Medical Costs Rise, More Americans Turn to Acupuncture," *Daily Finance*, April 2, 2011.
Sam Lister	"Celebrities Named and Shamed for Crazy Comments in the Name of Science," *Times Online*, January 4, 2010. http://women.timesonline.co.uk.
London Daily Mail Online	"Alternative Medicine Sales Soar as Consumers Shake Off Cynicism," January 26, 2010. www.dailymail.co.uk.
Dean Ornish	"Why Health Care Works Better than Disease Care," *Atlantic*, June 20, 2011.
Shalmali Pal	"Complementary Medicine Popular with Healthcare Workers," MedPage Today, August 19, 2011. www.medpagetoday.com.
Physician's Weekly	"Most Americans Using Alternative Therapies: *Consumer Reports*," August 5, 2011. www.physiciansweekly.com.
David Whelan	"A Panel of Medical Experts, Skillfully Refuted by *Playboy* Playmate Jenny McCarthy," *Science Business: Research, Innovation & Policy*, January 5, 2010. http://blogs.forbes.com.

CHAPTER 3

Can Alternative and Conventional Medicine Work Together?

Chapter Preface

According to the *Harvard Women's Health Watch*, "Tai chi is often described as 'meditation in motion,' but it might well be called '*medication* in motion.' There is growing evidence that this mind-body practice, which originated in China as a martial art, has value in treating or preventing many health problems."[1] Indeed, tai chi classes are commonly offered through hospital-affiliated exercise programs and dozens of research studies have been conducted to determine tai chi's effectiveness as a treatment for various conditions, including arthritis, diabetes, insomnia, and Parkinson's disease, as well as its positive effects on overall health, especially among older adults, for whom it has been found to be "an economic and effective exercise program for improving balance and balance confidence."[2]

While some forms of alternative therapies are not embraced by mainstream medicine, tai chi, because of its slow, gentle qualities, has been widely recommended by physicians as a method for reducing stress and for increasing physical activity. Tai chi has been associated with decreased incidence of chronic health conditions like heart disease and diabetes, and with better outcomes for patients recovering from cancer treatments like chemotherapy and surgery. A study of a special form of tai chi developed for diabetes patients failed to yield the hoped-for improvements in such measures as treatment compliance and fitness, but rather than dismissing the benefits of tai chi outright, researchers concluded that the modified form of tai chi "may not have been of sufficient intensity, frequency, or duration to effect positive changes in many aspects of physiology or health status relevant to older people with diabetes."[3] And a review of randomized controlled trials (RCTs) of both tai chi and qigong (a system of exercise, movement, and meditation with similarities to tai

114

chi) concluded that "research has demonstrated consistent, significant results for a number of health benefits."[4] In a randomized controlled trial, tai chi was shown to reduce the symptoms of fibromyalgia, described as "a common and complex clinical syndrome characterized by chronic and widespread musculoskeletal pain, fatigue, sleep disturbance, and physical and psychological impairment."[5] The authors of this study added: "This randomized, controlled trial shows that tai chi is potentially a useful therapy for patients with fibromyalgia," and concluded that their "results are consistent with those of a previous, nonrandomized trial of tai chi for fibromyalgia, as well as with the findings in other studies showing the benefits of tai chi with regard to musculoskeletal pain, depression, and quality of life."

The medical community's increasing interest in the use of tai chi as an adjunct to traditional disease treatment is just one example of the many ways in which alternative and conventional medicine can work together to improve patients' health and quality of life. The viewpoints in this chapter of *Opposing Viewpoints: Alternative Medicine* provide discussion of the field of integrative medicine, in which conventional doctors collaborate directly with alternative medicine practitioners on patient care; the role of integrative medicine as part of American health care reform; the potential cost savings for employers and insurers of making alternative therapies such as acupuncture and meditation available to employees; the scientific evidence supporting or refuting the effectiveness of alternative treatments; and the role of the placebo effect in both alternative and conventional medicine.

Notes

1. "The Health Benefits of Tai Chi," *Harvard Women's Health Watch*, May 2009.

2. H. Liu, A. Frank, "Tai Chi as a Balance Improvement Exercise for Older Adults: a Systematic Review," *Journal of Geriatric Physical Therapy*, vol. 33, no. 3, July–September 2010, p. 103.

3. T. Tsang, R. Orr, P. Lam, E.J. Comino, and M.F. Singh, "Health Benefits of Tai Chi for Older Patients with Type 2 Diabetes: The 'Move It For Diabetes Study'—A Randomized Controlled Trial," *Journal of Clinical Interventions in Aging*, vol. 2, no. 3, 2007, p. 429.

4. R. Jahnke, L. Larkey, C. Rogers, J. Etnier, and F. Lin, "A Comprehensive Review of Health Benefits of Qigong and Tai Chi," *American Journal of Health Promotion*, vol. 24, no. 6, July–August 2010, p. e1.

5. Chenchen Wang, Christopher H. Schmid, Ramel Rones, Robert Kalish, Janeth Yinh, Don L. Goldenberg, Yoojin Lee, and Timothy McAlindon, "A Randomized Trial of Tai Chi for Fibromyalgia," *New England Journal of Medicine*, vol. 363, no. 8, August 18, 2010, pp. 751–52.

> *"The sources of suffering are in sepa-*
> *rateness, . . . and the remedy is in re-*
> *membering that we are in this together.*
> *Integration, if it is to thrive, is the*
> *name of a duty to contribute what we*
> *can to a troubled and suffering planet."*

The Need for Improvements in Health Care Highlights the Advantages of Integrative Medicine

Donald Berwick (and Andrea M. Schultz, Samantha M. Chao, J. Michael McGinnis)

Andrea M. Schultz and Samantha M. Chao are associate pro-gram officers for the Institute of Medicine of the National Acad-emies, J. Michael McGinnis is a senior scholar for the institute, and Donald Berwick is a medical doctor who was the president and chief executive officer of the Institute for Healthcare Im-provement; in 2010 he was appointed by President Barack Obama as the administrator of the Centers for Medicare and

Medicaid Services. In the following viewpoint, the authors provide a transcript of Berwick's keynote address at the 2009 summit of the Institute of Medicine, in which Berwick promoted the benefits of creating a standard model for integrative medicine's core principles and patient-centered care to better address the problems facing the current American health care system and to facilitate a unified approach to improving patient service across the health care industry. Berwick defines what is meant by patient-centeredness and explains how this model, which encourages patients to take an active role in their care and focuses on an individualized approach, results in better health outcomes, greater patient satisfaction, and overall cost savings. Berwick emphasizes the health benefits realized by putting patients at the center of the care model, adapting treatments to each individual's needs, including patients' families and loved ones in the care process, and identifying ways in which patients can help themselves minimize the negative impact of illness and improve their overall health with changes to their daily lives.

As you read, consider the following questions:

1. What does Berwick indicate is the first challenge for integrative care?

2. What views of health care excellence make up the "Triple Aim," according to Berwick?

3. How does the Maori health care system in New Zealand define health quality, according to the viewpoint?

In his remarks, [Donald] Berwick, who leads the Institute for Healthcare Improvement, reflected on the array of earlier presentations and discussions [that took place during the February 2009 Summit on Integrative Medicine and the Health of the Public], focusing on the elements of integration that emphasize patient-centeredness and smooth care transitions. He endorsed the Rorschach metaphor used . . . by Dr. Harvey

Fineberg [to convey the idea that defining integrative medicine can be like viewing an inkblot called a Rorschach test, which people interpret in many different ways], saying that the speakers and audience were using a set of rather vaguely defined terms with great intention and wonderful spirit. However, he observed, these broad concepts of integrative medicine were being interpreted according to the individual backgrounds and needs of the participants. To make sense of the ambiguity around the terms and their usage, Berwick looked for the common purpose that pulled such diverse participants together, a purpose on which models of integrative medicine could be designed and built.

Despite the participants' enthusiastic support for integrative medicine, the simple notion of common purposes could prove to be a weak foundation for unity. The weakest foundation would be to unite based on a shared claim to a piece of a limited pie, said Berwick. A quest for greater reimbursement, for more payment for integrative care and alternative forms of care, may unite integrative medicine proponents today, but would soon divide them, as different groups assert their individual claims.

Professionals do need to be compensated for their services so that they can continue to carry out the work they love, he said. However, that goal is not a sufficient rallying point for building the cohesiveness necessary to advance integrative medicine. This movement must find a deeper offer to make to society. "Guilds are like mushrooms, and they will grow very fast before our eyes," he said. If integrative medicine becomes only a new list of guilds vying for reimbursement and organizational and professional power, "then we are wasting our time." Our health care system already has had too much negative experience with fragmentation, separation, and combat for a piece of the health care dollar. Thus, the first challenge for integrative care will be for the field to define what is being integrated, why, and then ultimately to integrate *itself*.

The Core Value: Patient-Centeredness

For nearly 20 years, committees of the Institute of Medicine [IOM] have recommended better system designs in health care. These efforts have addressed traditional allopathic care, curative care, end-of-life care, and now the important new arena of integrative health care. This body of work is exemplified by IOM's quality of care initiatives that have included the Roundtable on Quality in the mid-1990s and the "Crossing the Quality Chasm" report in 2001, both of which Berwick participated in. These efforts also grappled with the question of underlying purpose: Should anything be better about American health care? If so, what should that be? The roundtable's answer emerged as a trio of generalizable problems: overuse, underuse, and misuse. It also developed a workable definition of quality: "The degree to which health services for individuals and populations increase the likelihood of desired health outcomes and are consistent with current professional knowledge."

The subsequent Committee on Quality of Health Care in America then built a framework for quality on the foundation developed by the roundtable. It went beyond overuse, underuse, and misuse to define a more ambitious agenda for the health care system. The committee concluded that, in order to achieve a system of excellence, the health system should have six goals: safety, effectiveness, patient-centeredness, timeliness, efficiency, and equity.

In the committee's early discussions, the list included patient control, rather than patient-centeredness. The change represented the tension and a compromise between those who thought health care should belong to the patient and those who thought patient decisions should be mediated by professionals who have knowledge and experience that patients do not possess. The term *patient-centeredness* was chosen to imply a partnership that includes dialog and shared control.

Berwick's Principles for Integrative Medicine

1. Place the patient at the center.
2. Individualize care.
3. Welcome family and loved ones.
4. Maximize healing influences within care.
5. Maximize healing influences outside care.
6. Rely on sophisticated, disciplined evidence.
7. Use all relevant capacities—waste nothing.
8. Connect helping influences with each other.

TAKEN FROM: Donald Berwick, Institute for Healthcare Improvement, 2009.

The committee also enumerated 10 rules to redesign health care processes. The third rule, titled "The patient as the source of control," says "Patients should be given the necessary information and the opportunity to exercise the degree of control they choose over health care decisions that affect them. The health system should be able to accommodate differences in patient preferences and encourage shared decision making." This backs away from the idea of patients having total control, but supports the need for them to have the steering wheel in their hands. The committee's message was that patient-centeredness is important not only because it helps achieve better functional outcomes and greater safety, but also that it is, in and of itself, *a property of good care.*

A Patient-Centered Model Resembles Other Consumer-Driven Service Models

Other organizations—the Dartmouth Institute for Health Policy Research, the Institute for Healthcare Improvement, and the Picker Institute, for example—began to expand the application of patient-centered care. The Picker Institute proposed that the very definition of quality lies through the patient's eyes. The Institute for Healthcare Improvement asks patients whether they can agree with the statement that their provider—whether it be physician, practice, or hospital—gives them "exactly the help I want and need, exactly when I want and need it," which delegates the very definition of excellence to the experience of the person served.

This is a high standard, but one deemed necessary in almost every other consumer industry. Modern health care did not begin with a patient-centered standard. Instead, the field remained rooted in concepts proposed by Eliot Freidson in the mid-1900s. Freidson theorized that professions like medicine reserve to themselves the authority to judge the quality of their own work. Society gives professionals that authority on the assumption that the profession will be altruistic, has knowledge the public does not and cannot have, and can regulate itself. Again, this is not the basis for consumer relationships in most other industries.

Berwick described how the model of patient-centeredness is being translated into practice in various settings—Mayo Clinic's emphasis on "the needs of the patient come first," of the statement that Boston's Parker Hill Hospital set above its door, authored by its CEO, Arthur Berarducci, "Every Patient is the Only Patient," or creation of the healing environments envisioned in the Planetree model of care. New work at the Institute for Healthcare Improvement focuses on three population-based views of excellence, constituting the so-called "Triple Aim"—judging the experience of care through the patient's eyes, addressing the health of the population served, and considering per capita cost as a measure of system quality.

Prior to recent decades and in many cultures worldwide, the dominant definition of health was, in essence, the extent to which the body can heal itself—physically, mentally and spiritually. In this view, the role of medicine and health care is that of a servant, an assistant to bodily processes already under way. Its job "is to let [the body] do so, to stand out of the way, and to offer resources or assets to allow [healing] to move forward," said Berwick. This conception adds to the significance of the patient-centeredness concept and begins to suggest what integrative medicine could mean and what its purpose is.

Achieving Integrative Medicine's Aims

Just as the IOM committee on quality defined a set of design principles that could realize its vision of quality care, certain design principles might move the health system toward more integrative care—"the care that connects technology to souls." Berwick shared a poignant personal anecdote that illustrated the ways in which right care needs to draw from the integration of personal values and priorities with clinical concerns. Drawing on the day's discussion, Berwick suggested eight such principles, summarized in [the box under "Berwick's Principles for Integrative Medicine"].

The first principle put forward was to *put the patient at the center*. Good examples of this are the chronic care model [emphasizing systemic change to preventive care and care for chronic illnesses so that the model emphasizes all of the elements of integrative care described by Berwick] developed by [Edward] Wagner, or the Mayo Clinic's "the needs of the patient come first."

Second, and related, is *individualization*. New technology, such as advances in genomics, makes the individualization of care ever more possible. Berwick predicted that a science-based, individually focused, predictive system of health and care could be the death knell for insurance as we know it today. Actuarial prediction of costs becomes impossible when "every patient is the only patient" and care is customized to the level of the individual.

Third, *welcome and embrace* the patient's family, loved ones, and community. This means not separating a person from the loving community that provides energy, self-esteem, solace, and wisdom. In today's hospitals, "We create nothing so reliably as we create loneliness," said Berwick. New Zealand's Maori health care system defines health quality as including physical health, emotional health, spiritual health, and family health. Such a definition emphasizes the essential value of connectedness.

Fourth, *maximize healing influences in health care facilities.* In other words, make current treatment facilities healing places by, for example, refocusing human interactions and using evidence-based designs that reduce patient, family, and staff stress; prevent errors and nosocomial [originating in a hospital] infections; and increase positive influences on health status.

Fifth, *maximize healing influences outside the care system.* This requires the system and providers to learn about and help patients implement the many actions they can take in their daily lives to heal themselves or minimize the impact of illness or disability. The formal system of care rarely considers these opportunities.

Sixth, *rely on sophisticated and disciplined evidence.* For an integrative system of care, this may be the most difficult challenge. It requires forms of evidence and approaches to learning that are far less developed and far less recognized today than canonical experimental designs and randomized trials. This is because, in the full expression of patient-centered, individualized, integrative care, each person is a continuous experiment of one, and rigorous measurement and evaluation need to be applied to individual learning cycles, over the long term. This type of research is not currently embraced by traditional research funders or scientific journals, Berwick noted. While patient-centered research needs to be every bit as robust and disciplined as current methods, it requires a forward leap in methodology to learn from the experience of the individual patient.

Seventh, *use all relevant capacities.* In a sense, the potential health care workforce is exactly as large as the entire population. The concept that we have a shortage in primary care is conditioned on a very limited view of the capacity of almost all human beings, said Berwick. Individual patients, their families, and even their community can have insights about the person's condition that formal care providers cannot.

Finally, *the importance of connection.* Potential helping influences must connect with one another. One strategy for this is through health navigators and health coaches. Another is through interconnected information systems. However, the fundamental generator of connection begins with an attitude of cooperation among all individuals and institutions involved in a person's care.

Durable, worthy connections among and across the many individuals and organizations supporting integrative medicine can be forged by rediscovering and affirming a common purpose: *what we wish to heal.* What we health care professionals wish to heal, Berwick suggested, are those who come to us for help; ourselves who are among them; a broken, imbalanced, greedy, technocentric, unself-conscious health care system; and a world that has displayed infinite cleverness in increasing human suffering. "The sources of suffering are in separateness," Berwick said, "and the remedy is in remembering that we are in this together. Integration, if it is to thrive, is the name of a duty to contribute what we can to a troubled and suffering planet."

> *"Though the studies are few, CAM therapies have the potential to offset serious medical costs for employers and employees."*

A Complementary Medical Treatment Approach Can Lower Health Care Costs

Kathleen Koster

Kathleen Koster is the online managing editor of Employee Benefit News. *In the following viewpoint, Koster reports that more and more health insurance providers and employers are offering coverage or discounts for complementary and alternative medicine (CAM) treatments, because research proves that these treatments, including chiropractic, nutritional therapies, acupuncture, and mind-body therapy, are effective in lowering overall health care costs and in reducing employees' absences from work. Because interest in and demand for alternative medicine treatments is widespread, Koster asserts, employers will have no trouble convincing their employees to take advantage of such benefits that will in turn significantly reduce disability costs and absenteeism. Koster cites a study conducted with twenty-five employees at a Ford Motor Company truck plant that found a statistically significant difference in reduction of pain between employees who received acupuncture treatments and training in meditation versus employees who received traditional care, consisting of physical therapy and medication. Koster reports that larger studies are needed to increase employees' access to alternative therapies, but she suggests that interest among employers is strong and growing stronger.*

As you read, consider the following questions:

1. What percentage of employers provided coverage for chiropractic care, according to a 2009 study cited in the viewpoint?

2. What type of interventions does Dr. Kenneth Pelletier emphasize as promising the greatest efficacy for the most individuals and for the widest number of medical conditions, according to the viewpoint?

3. What factor, besides its limited size, does Walter J. Talamonti say reduced the power of the Ford Motor Company study, according to the viewpoint?

Complementary and alternative medicine (CAM) treatments are all the rage lately for consumers, and many [health insurance] carriers are catching on to the trend by offering discounts on or coverage of certain benefits.

[Health insurance company] Cigna's Healthy Rewards discount program includes discounts for acupuncture, chiropractic care and massage, as well as natural supplements and many other health and wellness products and services.

Wendy Sherry, Cigna's vice president of product development, explains that CAM has the potential to lower traditional health care costs.

"For example, targeted use of chiropractic care to treat the back and spine can cost less than surgery. Using acupuncture instead of anesthesia can also cost less," Sherry says. "However, these are unproven approaches, which is why Cigna does not cover them as standard benefits."

"On the other hand," she continues, "when the benefits are not limited in some way—for example, with an annual maximum number of visits—people could use the treatment when it's not medically necessary, which is beyond the scope of health insurance coverage. That could drive up claim costs. It is also costly to manually manage claim reviews on alternative medicine benefits to ensure medical necessity."

Research Shows Health Benefits and Cost Savings with Complementary Treatment

Dr. Kenneth R. Pelletier, professor at the University of Arizona school of medicine and the University of California at San Francisco School of Medicine, disagrees.

"Yes [these alternative medicines should be offered as part of a comprehensive health benefit package] because there is good evidence in favorable clinical outcomes, and in the cases where there has been a cost-benefit analysis or a return on investment, the results are very promising," says Pelletier, who is also the chairman of the American Health Association and is a vice president with Healthtrac Incorporated.

He explains that by offering these alternative treatments under a benefit plan, employees return to work sooner and experience fewer relapses. Also, medical costs tend to flatten relative to what they would have been.

The most common and effective treatments include chiropractic, nutritional therapies, acupuncture and mind-body therapy. Research shows that acupuncture, for example, was present in 24% of company benefit plans, and only 26% of employers offered no alternative care benefits.

Chiropractic care, for which 72% of employers provided coverage in a 2009 Mercer study, for the limbs, joints or back pain is more cost effective in comparison to the usual care regimen.

According to an October 2009 [A.] Milstein [and N.] Choudry report that measured the effectiveness of chiropractic care in treating low-back pain and neck pain, this type of care not only was medically beneficial, but also cost effective.

"[The authors of this study] felt that chiropractic care would be a clinically effective and cost-effective intervention to shift away from the traditional medical care and physical therapy care. Relative to the neck pain environment, their comment was that it would be highly cost effective," says Dr. Gerard Clum, president of Life Chiropractic College West. The researchers concluded that using chiropractic care in the lower back region would be cost effective and would save a significant amount of money in treating neck pain.

The Center for Health Value Innovation [CHVI] used the Milstein report as a key element to develop its own report released at a May 2010 summit. CHVI implemented feedback from the 2009 study into the matrix to be evaluated from a value-based approach to health benefits.

"Their perspective was that chiropractic hasn't been evaluated in a value-based design perspective and if it were, it could have significant positive impact in terms of cost and patient outcomes," Clum explains.

CHVI also found that chiropractic care had the potential for significant savings, which leads Clum to conclude: "I don't think there's any question" that chiropractic services can lower traditional health cost for neck pain and low-back pain claims.

Convincing Company Leadership to Offer Complementary Treatment by Illustrating Evidence of Effectiveness and Cost Savings

When convincing upper management to cover chiropractic care or other complementary treatments in a company's benefits package, HR/benefits pros should show them the evidence, Clum advises.

Implementing CAM treatments such as chiropractic care can reduce disability costs and absenteeism.

On the other hand, convincing employees is not a significant obstacle because of popular consumer demand.

"The consumer uptake for chiropractics has been tremendous, and frankly that's what's driven the industry for decades. The consumer demand has been there, but the system demand to respond to that has been what's lagged," says Clum.

Nutritional therapies also are popular and may be monitored by a registered dietician for weight loss, heart disease prevention, or recoveries from heart surgery.

Acupuncture for back pain or postoperative pain also is generally coded and billed with most insurers covering it, says Pelletier. When treating some forms of acute pain, it can be less expensive than surgery, implants, or electrodes.

Further, mind-body therapy, relaxation, or martial arts such as tai chi (which is probably not covered, even though studies have shown its positive outcomes for problems like heart disease and chronic pain) can be other considerations for employers looking into CAM.

Mind-body interventions have the greatest efficacy for the largest amount of people for the greatest variety of medical conditions, Pelletier emphasizes. It's also very inexpensive to deliver, while addressing a vast array of problems such as chronic pain, stress, and depression. He says that most insurers cover these benefits if embedded in a stress management program. It's important to read over your plan coverage, as the carrier may cover this treatment though it may not be named.

The Ford Motor Company Experience with Complementary Medicine

For their workers' compensation program, Ford Motor Company experimented with alternative medicine such as acupuncture and mind-body meditation.

The worksite assessment started in 2006 and was published in March of 2010. It studied workers at a Louisville, Ky., truck plant who complained of acute lower-back pain under workers' compensation.

Employees were divided into two groups: The control group received the usual care in the on-site clinic, which prescribed medication if needed and physical therapy. The second group received the usual care in addition to the intervention care, which entailed weekly acupuncture treatments and the Healthyroads program, in which participants were taught meditation skills to aid relaxation and help overcome pain.

The 25 total participants were reviewed at six and 10 weeks with a number of tests, which measured perceived pain and depression levels, among other metrics.

Researchers found that there was small, but statistically significant, improvement in pain findings in the experimental group over the control group.

Further, participants in the intervention group were using significantly fewer opiates or other treatments than those on standard protocol at six weeks. There also was a marginally significant reduction in physical therapy among those using complementary medicine in addition to the traditional regimen.

When asked whether complementary medicine can lower traditional health cost claims, Walter J. Talamonti, medical director of clinical operations at Ford Motor Company, explains that "you can't make that [determination] at this point. That's a big jump." He adds that a formal study with more patients to measure would be needed to form an opinion.

Further Study Is Needed on the Initial Positive Outcomes of Complementary Treatments

Still, the findings from his observations at the Kentucky plant are promising. Employees can't work on the plant floor if they are taking narcotics for pain, so a program like Healthyroads or an acupuncture regimen may help them get back on the job sooner. They're considering another study on the effect of complementary medicine on injuries to the upper extremities as soon as next year.

When proposing the study, Talamonti used an evidence-based approach for getting permission from upper management. His hope for the pilot was to prove the efficacy of these alternative medicines definitively, but not enough people participated.

For this reason, although they may send an employee covered under workers' comp to an acupuncturist, these benefits are not yet covered under the general benefits package.

"We need to divide out [the treatments] and do a large study," he says. "Once we have the proper data, if it does work, then we have something that can be peer reviewed, published and therefore be able to implement it.

"If you're looking at evidence-based [programs] and you have to justify the cost, you would have a difficult time justifying it to upper management as to why you're doing this."

Ultimately, there was not enough power in the study because there were too few people, and you can't tease apart the impact of acupuncture and meditation, he explains. Nevertheless, he believes that they're headed in the right direction with these interesting findings.

"We'd like to continue looking at this, particularly for the upper extremities, but it will probably take more than one facility to get enough people to give the study adequate power," concludes Talamonti.

Though the studies are few, CAM therapies have the potential to offset serious medical costs for employers and employees.

"It's time to relook at everything to do with health care," says Clum. "Rearranging the deck chairs on *Titanic* is not going to help the ship. We need to take a hard look at what we're getting for the dollars that we're spending and explore if [there are] ways that we haven't normally thought of as a first course of action that could be more reasonable, more appropriate clinically and economically of the future of business, as well as the future of the consumer."

> "Science does not make assertions about what cannot be true, simply because evidence that it is true has not yet been generated. Science does not mistake absence of evidence for evidence of absence. Science itself is fluid."

A Complementary Approach to Medicine Helps Patients and Is Scientifically Sound

David Katz

David Katz is a medical doctor, the founding director of Yale University's Prevention Research Center, the editor in chief of the journal Childhood Obesity, *and the author of several books including* Nutrition in Clinical Practice *and* The Flavor Full Diet. *In the following viewpoint, Katz rejects the claims of critics who depict him as a proponent of unproven, pseudoscientific alternative medicine therapies. Katz points to publicly available records of his participation in legitimate research trials and his publication of more than 120 peer-reviewed papers to verify his credentials as an experienced, accredited medical expert and sci-*

entist. He also mentions several studies, conducted at the research lab that he has run for a decade and a half, which did not support the use of various alternative medicine modalities for the conditions studied—such as a study that his research group published that showed that yoga was not an effective supplementary treatment for asthma—as evidence that not only does research on complementary and alternative medicine (CAM) treatments follow strict scientific protocols, but also it is unbiased. Katz states that his commitment is not to CAM, but to healing his patients, and that he uses what he calls the CARE (clinical applications of research evidence) construct as a guideline for determining whether or not to recommend a given CAM or conventional treatment. Katz explains that he became interested in CAM treatments when he was unable to help his patients get better using conventional medicine, and he maintains that integrative medicine greatly expands the treatment options available to clinicians and patients.

As you read, consider the following questions:

1. For what condition does Katz indicate massage therapy is a promising treatment?

2. According to Katz, what five domains does the CARE construct suggest are important to any clinical decision?

3. Of what "club" does Katz say he is a card-carrying member?

Friends recently brought to my attention a commentary in the *Atlantic* in which the following is said about me, purportedly related to a presentation I gave at Yale:

> "... [He] listed a lot of things he'd tried and which failed to work. His conclusion was not that they should be abandoned, but that we needed 'a more fluid concept of evidence.'"

Those same friends know me, of course, so they, along with anyone else who knows me, know this characterization to be incorrect.

The troubling thing is how easy it would have been for the author to know it, too. He either didn't know it, which means he is making very public assertions without even doing a rudimentary amount of homework; or he knew it and willfully misrepresented my position. Neither is to his credit.

Publicly Available Records Illustrate a History of Unbiased Scientific Research

My professional activities have turned me into a fairly public figure, so my life's work is an open book, at the disposal of anyone with Internet access. My publication record in the peer-reviewed literature is accessible to all in two simple steps: go to PubMed.gov, and type "Katz DL" into the search box. Three steps, if clicking "go" counts.

What that record, along with my CV [curriculum vitae] (which is also readily available online . . .) shows is that the statement in the *Atlantic* is nonsense.

I have run a research lab for roughly 15 years, secured and managed approximately $30 million in research funding, and published more than 120 peer-reviewed papers. Among those papers are reports of studies in complementary and alternative medicine [CAM], the alleged threat to science the commentator in the *Atlantic* and other self-proclaimed "guardians of science," oppose.

But doing science is not, and cannot be, a threat to science. We have studied complementary and alternative medicine modalities with an open mind and unbiased methods. So, for instance, we have shown that massage therapy does indeed appear to be a very promising treatment for osteoarthritis. Our research in that area is ongoing.

But we have also shown that chromium supplementation does not appear to be effective in treating insulin resistance.

In direct contradiction to the allegation in the *Atlantic*, the results of our own research along with the weight of evidence have, of course, prompted us to stop using chromium supplements for this purpose. We published evidence, at odds with our hopes, indicating that yoga is not effective adjuvant therapy for asthma. Why would anyone continue to use what doesn't work?

We have shown that meditation combined with massage improves quality of life in end-stage AIDS [acquired immunodeficiency syndrome]. We have shown that homeopathy does not effectively treat ADHD [attention-deficit/hyperactivity disorder] in children. We have studied intravenous nutrients for fibromyalgia, and are as yet uncertain about the therapeutic effect.

There is additional nonsense attributed to me. I allegedly believe in "mysterious forces." My actual belief? There are no mysterious forces; there are just forces that exist, such as osmolarity, gravity and electromagnetism. Some forces that exist we understand well; some we understand poorly; and some, no doubt, are as yet undiscovered and we don't understand them at all.

I also, allegedly, believe in spoon-bending. (My actual view, of course, is courtesy of the education I received in [the science fiction film] *The Matrix*: There is no spoon! The jury is still out on forks . . .)

A Rigid Conception of Evidence Is Unscientific and Does Not Serve Patients' Needs

If the guardians contend that under the expansive rubrics of "CAM" and "integrative medicine" there is nonsense and charlatanism, they are of course correct. If because of that they contend that nothing legitimate can be done under those banners, they might look more closely at the glass walls of the houses of conventional medicine before throwing such stones.

The guardians contend that CAM is all about lies, and its practitioners all authorized, and inclined, to lie to their patients. But telling a patient "I will never stop trying to find something to make you feel better" is neither a lie, nor a false promise, nor a source of false hope (if, indeed, one never does stop trying). The promise, and the hope, are then real.

I am by no means a CAM zealot. In fact, I never had any particular interest in being involved in CAM. I always have, however, had an abiding interest in helping my patients get better.

A commitment to patients should not attenuate one's devotion to science and evidence. But it does require—wait for it!—that notorious "more fluid" concept of evidence! This, according to the guardians of science, puts us into the realm of what they call "woo." Does it really?

Of course not. Fluidity is simply the opposite of rigidity. A rigid view of evidence is that it works like a light switch: on/off, pure illumination versus utter darkness. Any true scientist would consider this sheer nonsense. Even the brilliance of Einstein's relativity theory is the subject of ongoing validations, decades after his death. Science itself is fluid, constantly flowing in accord with new and better theories, new and better evidence.

The CARE Construct

What, exactly, is this dangerous "fluidity" I espouse? Actually, it is represented by a construct we have published on a number of occasions, and which I have presented at an Institute of Medicine summit. I call the construct CARE, standing for "clinical applications of research evidence."

The CARE construct suggests that there are 5 domains important to any clinical decision: safety, efficacy, research, preference, and alternatives. The construct is best illuminated by looking at the two extremes of its range.

Imagine a therapy that is perfectly safe, highly effective, supported by unassailable research, is just what the patient wants, and that faces no competition from any other therapy that can do the same job. Are there any doubts about the prudence of this choice?

At the other end of the range is a treatment that is likely dangerous, probably ineffective, and lacking good evidence, about which the patient is ambivalent, and for which there are safer, more effective, better studied alternatives. Any questions what to do in this situation?

The far-more-common clinical scenario, however, is in between. Consider a therapy that appears to be safe. There are indications in the literature that it might be effective. There is some relevant research, but no definitive clinical trials. The patient has tried everything that is routinely recommended for their condition, and is not better—and wants to try "something else." There is not something else to try that is safer or better substantiated than the therapy under consideration.

The CARE construct, along with an awareness that evidence is not limited to flavors of "iron clad" or "absent," suggests that a promising but uncertain therapy is, indeed, the reasonable next thing to try in a patient who has already tried more conventional therapies which have failed. Take this incremental step along the spectrum of evidence, and you are into the realm of integrative medicine—no hucksterism or false promises required.

This is what I presented at Yale. This is what I practice. Apparently getting one's facts straight is not a prerequisite to writing commentaries in the *Atlantic*.

Integrative Medicine Helps Doctors and Patients Overcome the Limits of Conventional Care

I have long been in the crosshairs of the self-professed "guardians of science." They have seen to it that I have been feath-

Complementary Treatments Can Increase Patient Compliance and Health Benefits

Given the prevalence of use and the favorable effects of complementary therapy observed in this analysis, there are reasons to believe that individuals experiencing beneficial effects likely have a greater commitment to and continue to rely on complementary therapies for health self-management. This may affect the content and quality of patient-provider interaction and adherence to prescribed therapies. The potential value of complementary therapies should not be discounted. Awareness of the potential benefits can help health providers better monitor and document complementary therapy use in medical charts, thus enabling providers to effectively support aging patients in making informed, safe, and appropriate choices.

Ha T. Nguyen, Joseph G. Grzywacz,
Wei Lang, Michael Walkup, and Thomas A. Arcury,
"Effects of Complementary Therapy on Health in a National
U.S. Sample of Older Adults," Journal of Alternative and
Complementary Medicine, *vol. 16, no. 7, July 20, 2010.*

ered, if not tarred, in cyberspace. Why? I maintain that responsiveness to the needs of patients is as great an imperative in medicine as responsible use of science. This is the basis on which I have been charged with quackery, and my position is: If this is quackery, I would rather be a duck than a doctor. Hence, the feathering.

I am, in fact, a card-carrying member of the evidence-based medicine club, and always have been. Among my publications is a textbook on evidence-based medicine which, if I may say so myself, is pretty good. It is from this foundation that I confidently assert that responsible use of science and responsiveness to the needs of patients that tend to go on even when the evidence base runs thin are not irreconcilable.

The inducement for me to practice integrative medicine was very straightforward and involved no eye of newt or voodoo rituals. As a primary care internist over a span of years, I simply had some patients I could not make better. Their pain did not go away, their migraines did not resolve, the medications that should have mitigated their various and sundry risk factors for chronic disease evoked intolerable side effects instead; their syndromes remained undiagnosable. This limitation was not specific testimony to my own clinical deficiencies—although I readily admit those, as any honest clinician must—because all such patients were referred to expert subspecialists. When such patients failed to get better, it wasn't just because I couldn't help them; it was despite the best that modern medicine could offer them.

So a simple dilemma presented itself: When the conventional treatments fail to help a patient, do you tell them "sorry, I tried" and leave them to their fate, or do you pledge to help them look beyond the conventional to try to find something that might work for them?

I chose the latter—still the road less traveled, many years later—and that, indeed, has made all the difference, most notably for the patients I have been able to help as a result. When the going in medicine gets tough, a clinician can tell their patient "tough luck," but that to me seems wrong. Instead, I believe we should tough it out by our patients' side, and help make decisions when the next logical thing to try is far from clear.

That's what we do in my practice, which is also a matter of public record. Those who choose to denigrate it from a distance are hereby extended an invitation to visit, and, with the patient's assent, to sit in as we do what we do. I will surrender myself immediately to the butterfly nets of the authorities if at any point they see an eye of newt change hands.

Attacks on Integrative Medicine Are Unproven and Scientifically Unsound

With that image fresh in my mind, I anticipate the guardians lifting lines from this very post to continue their case against me. I hope they have fun. Assuming they get the quote right in the first place (really, how hard is that?), the rest of us will know the importance of context.

Someone might be quoted as saying "I believe I can fly." That might mean the person has decompensated schizophrenia. It might mean they've used LSD. But it also might mean they are a steely-eyed ninja airline pilot who not only *can* fly, but can land a crippled airliner in the Hudson River without injuring anyone, too! I rest my case for context.

Writing this is, inevitably, apt to seem an act of self-defense, and like all self-defense, to appear defensive. But to be honest, the guardians of science have done me no discernible harm despite their best efforts, and years of unsubstantiated allegations. So while I suppose I am indulging in some self-defense, I am far more concerned with defending science. Because the self-proclaimed guardians of science are denigrating it, every day.

Some of them critique research, without conducting any. Others critique patient care, never having cared for a patient. With friends like these, the public surely needs no enemies.

They reach conclusions about where I (and presumably others) stand without the careful review of my track record a scientific accounting would require. I have actually "mapped" the evidence base underlying complementary and alternative therapies, inventing a method in the process that has been adopted by the World Health Organization. They reach conclusions about the nature of my clinical practice, never having visited my clinic, and thus defiling the principle of direct observation on which all good science is based.

Science is advanced by an open mind that seeks knowledge, while acknowledging its current limits. Science does not make assertions about what cannot be true, simply because evidence that it is true has not yet been generated. Science does not mistake absence of evidence for evidence of absence. Science itself is fluid.

Science does not make assertions about what must be true when the evidence for it is in flux. Science does not espouse absolute knowledge, and scientists dutifully resist the tendency to fall in love with their own preconceived notions. Science subjects itself to the scientific method, which sometimes validates what one wishes to be true, and other times refutes it. A scientist accepts the results, whether hoped for or otherwise.

The self-proclaimed guardians of science are, in actuality, peddlers of propaganda. They practice their craft with a blend of sanctimony and hypocrisy, and violate the scientific method to advance their own notoriety. They make routine use of the term "woo" because it can mean whatever they want it to mean—a decidedly unscientific practice.

They "defend" science with an apparently blind faith, a selective approach to information, neglect of firsthand observation, lack of due diligence, and a religious fervor hinting at fanaticism. As such, their defense of science is an insult to science. Applying religious fervor to science is, at best, oxymoronic—give or take the "oxy."

> *"Physicians who for the sake of funding embrace and endorse unscientific views and practices under the guise of CAM or integrative medicine, do so knowing that they often contradict the established principles of physics, chemistry, and biology."*

Complementary Medicine Is Scientifically Unsound and Only Increases Provider Profits

Ben Kavoussi

Ben Kavoussi has a master's degree in oriental medicine, is a licensed acupuncturist, and is a regular contributor to Science-Based Medicine, a website that focuses on exposing what it views as conflicts between science and alternative medical treatments. In the following viewpoint, Kavoussi derides physicians and university medical centers who, in the name of profit over medical science, accept research grant funds to conduct studies on alternative medical treatments that they know, according to Kavoussi, are unsupported by scientific measures. Kavoussi details several research trials conducted by teams at California-based university medical centers that are, he declares, guilty of knowingly promoting "snake oil," or fake medical treatments. The author also cites an example of a case in which a published study that purported to have found clinical evidence of the link between an acupuncture needle point and a particular area of the brain was later retracted when another study was published that revealed that a correlation between acupuncture points and the brain could not be identified and that, in fact, no correlation could be identified between specific acupuncture points and any perceived reduction in pain. Kavoussi refers to a 2009 post that he authored in which he illustrated that traditional Chinese medicine did not include acupuncture, which was first introduced in the twentieth century. Traditional Chinese medicine, Kavoussi declares, was similar to the medicine practiced by early Europeans and involved such practices as lancing and bloodletting.

As you read, consider the following questions:

1. What year was UCSF's Osher Center for Integrative Medicine established, according to Kavoussi?

2. How much was given by Henry and Susan Samueli to the University of California, Irvine in 2000 to fund research on acupuncture, herbal therapy, and ayurveda, according to the viewpoint?

3. What treatment method does Kavoussi say played a prominent role in the national health care system under the Chinese Communist Party?

All the world sees us
In grand style wherever we are;
The big and the small
Are infatuated with us:

They run to our remedies
And regard us as gods
And to our prescriptions
Principles and regimens, they sub-
mit themselves.

Molière,
The Imaginary Invalid (1673)

The passage above is part of a burlesque doctoral confer-
ment ceremony, where the French playwright Molière
(1622–1673) mocks the unscrupulous physicians of his time.
"All the excellency of their art consists in pompous gibberish,
in a specious babbling, which gives you words instead of reasons, and promises instead of results," he writes. In Molière's
plays doctors never cure anyone; they are put on stage just to
display their own vanity and ignorance. The Spanish painter
Francisco de Goya (1746–1828) also took on the same issue
by painting in 1799 a well-attired jackass taking the pulse of a
dying man, in a pose that accentuates the large gem on his
hoof.

Integrative Medicine Research Centers Value Money over Science and Patients' Interests

But if the asinine doctors of Molière and de Goya's time never
cured anyone, it is because they held pre-scientific views, and
believed that disease was caused by imbalances in "humors,"
and by malefic [evil] influences of the Heavens. Even the most
educated among them treated illnesses in good faith by purg-
ing, bloodletting, and enema at astrologically auspicious times.
In contrast, current physicians who for the sake of funding
embrace and endorse unscientific views and practices under
the guise of CAM [complementary and alternative medicine]
or integrative medicine, do so knowing that they often contradict the established principles of physics, chemistry, and biol-

ogy. Therefore, in addition to promoting "snake oil science" (as R. Barker Bausell calls it [in his 2007 book, *Snake Oil Science: The Truth About Complementary and Alternative Medicine*]), these physicians are also guilty of bad faith. Most of this takes place at large academic centers, where funding seems to outweigh the concern for science. As Val Jones, MD, writes in "2009's Top 5 Threats to Science in Medicine":

> Often referred to by David Gorski as "Quackademic" Medical Centers—there is a growing trend among these centers to accept endowments for "integrative" approaches to medical care. Because of the economic realities of decreasing healthcare reimbursements—these once proud defenders of science are now accepting money to "study" implausible and often disproven medical treatments because they're trendy. Scientists at these centers are forced to look the other way while patients (who trust the center's reputation that took tens of decades to build) are exposed to placebo medicine under the guise of "holistic" healthcare.

A list of these centers, available at the Academic Woo Aggregator website, reveals the prestigious University of California (UC) as the most represented, with 3 centers: the UCSF [University of California, San Francisco] Osher Center for Integrative Medicine; the Susan Samueli Center for Integrative Medicine at UC Irvine; and the Collaborative Centers for Integrative Medicine at UCLA [University of California, Los Angeles], which includes the Center for East-West Medicine. The William R. Pritchard Veterinary Medical Teaching Hospital at UC Davis, with its acupuncture and traditional Chinese veterinary medicine (TCVM) clinic, should perhaps be added to the list.

Among them, UCSF's Osher Center for Integrative Medicine has the largest funding, with a cumulative sum of over $28 million. Established in 1997 by the Dean Emeritus of the School of Medicine, Haile T. Debas, MD, and the very generous support of the Bernard Osher Foundation, the UCSF center collaborates with Harvard University, and the Karolinska Institute in Stockholm.

Some of the "integrative" medicine research involves acupuncture, even if it might end up being a source of scientific embarrassment. Consider, for instance, the dubious research during the 1990s at UC Irvine by the physicist Zang-Hee Cho, who claimed to have *in vivo* evidence by fMRI [functional magnetic resonance imaging] for acupuncture's putative [supposed] effects. Cho and his colleagues published a series of papers, notably one in the *Proceedings of the National Academy of Sciences* (PNAS), where they claimed to have observed a correlation between the visual cortex and an acupuncture point on the toe. Based on this unconfirmed observation, they became persuaded that acupuncture involves the activation of the cortical region associated with the targeted organ. Cho went as far as claiming that the cortical activation depends on the subject's personality type, which could be *yin* or *yang*! Fortunately, the PNAS article, which is often referenced by acupuncture apologists, was retracted in June 2006 by Cho himself and a number of its coauthors:

> Accumulating evidence suggests that the central nervous system is essential for processing these effects, via its modulation of the autonomic nervous system, neuro-immune system, and hormonal regulation. We, therefore, carried out a series of studies questioning whether there really is point specificity in acupuncture, especially vis-à-vis pain and acupuncture analgesic [pain-relieving] effects as we originally reported in our PNAS article, that had not yet been confirmed by other studies. . . . Having concluded that there is no point specificity, at least for pain and analgesic effects, and that we no longer agree with the results in our PNAS article, the undersigned authors are retracting the article.
>
> Z.H. Cho
>
> S.C. Chung

H.J. Lee

E.K. Wong

B.I. Min

Cho has since left the University of California, and is now the director of the Neuroscience Research Institute at Gachon University of Medicine and Science in Korea. However, his research lead to a $5.7 million gift to UC Irvine in 2000 by Henry and Susan Samueli to research acupuncture, herbal therapy, and the "Indian science of life," ayurveda. This funding was used to create the Susan Samueli Center for Integrative Medicine.

UCLA Wastes Resources on Acupuncture in Pursuit of Funding

UCLA's "integrative" medicine also involves acupuncture. Although several separate groups and individuals provide acupuncture at UCLA, most of it is now centralized at the Center for East-West Medicine, which was founded in 1993 by its current director, Ka-Kit Hui, MD. The center's website states that in March 2005, the Annenberg Foundation awarded $2 million to UCLA to establish the Wallis Annenberg Endowed Chair in Integrative East-West Medicine. An additional $115,790 grant allowed for the creation of a "healing environment." Meanwhile, the center is using UCLA's international fame to lend legitimacy to Chinese folk medicine. Take a peek at *UCLA Today* of June 17, 2010:

> Representing a 5,000-year history of traditional Chinese medicine, Chinese Vice Minister of Health Dr. Wang Guo-qiang and a six-person delegation came to campus June 11 to see what they could learn from UCLA, which has long been at the forefront of research in integrative medicine and education in the Western world. . . . The Chinese delegation, which had a four-day stay in the U.S., chose UCLA as the

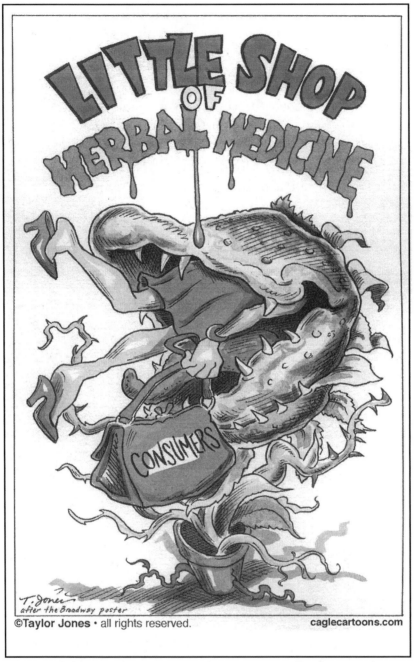

© 2010 by Taylor Jones, Hoover Digest. Cagle Cartoons, Inc. All rights reserved.

only academic medical center to visit to learn how traditional Chinese medicine (TCM) and integrative medicine are practiced as a new health care model. . . . Wang is the highest-ranking official in China overseeing the development of Chinese medicine and integrated medicine.

Now read the following grim news about UCLA's budget, announced just three months before, which might put the arrival of the Chinese delegation in a whole new perspective. *UCLA Today* wrote on Feb 18, 2010, that:

In planning for next year's budget, campus leaders believe that UCLA will face a permanent loss of $117 million in state funding for 2010–11, the same as in 2009–10, but with one difference. The $55 million cut that was made on a one-time basis in 2009–10 will become permanent. . . . And although Gov. Arnold Schwarzenegger seeks to restore the one-time $305 million reduction made to UC's budget this fiscal year—$55 million of which was cut from UCLA's budget—campus leaders said they are assuming that the state legislature is going to reject his proposal.

With UCLA experiencing an unprecedented drop in state support, even snake oil science is welcomed, as long as it leads to further funding prospects. After all, as the Roman Emperor Vespasian once said: *Pecunia non olet* (money does not smell).

In my 2009 post "Astrology with Needles," I presented images from European manuals of bloodletting, which clearly indicate that the acclaimed 5,000-year history of traditional Chinese medicine does not include acupuncture as we know it today. What the Chinese practiced is lancing and bloodletting with bodkins and lancets, which significantly resembled what Europeans and Muslims also practiced. This is why the venipuncture points portrayed in European medieval manuscripts significantly overlap with key points described in the Chinese classics. In addition, the evidence presented in my recent post, "The Acupuncture and Fasciae Fallacy," shows that the tools described in the Chinese classics resemble fleams and other venipuncture instruments of medieval Europe, and have little resemblance to what is currently considered an acupuncture needle. This is because acupuncture with fine needles is a modern invention; one that was transformed from a sidelined practice of the early 20th century to an essential and high-profile part of the national health care system under the Chinese Communist Party.

Finally, the visit of the Chinese delegation to UCLA reminds me of a 1998 French film called *The Dinner Game* (*Le dîner de cons*). In it, Pierre and his Parisian friends organize a dinner party each week, where everyone invites the most ridiculous character he can find, so they can all have a good time mocking him. But when Pierre invites François, who he thinks will steal the show, his clueless guest inadvertently exposes hidden and embarrassing aspects of Pierre's life. The visitors that have come to UCLA to represent 5,000 years of hocus-pocus, and are eager to learn about an integrative medicine that is mainly a showcase to obtain funding, might have—like François—unknowingly exposed a mockery, and with it, a great charade.

> *"Even at this preliminary stage in the research, however, it's clear that it's time to flip our ideas about fake pills upside down."*

Doctors Can and Should Regularly Use Ethically Prescribed Placebo Treatments

Steve Silberman

Steve Silberman is the author of the blog NeuroTribes *and a science journalist who has contributed articles and interviews to several periodicals, including* Wired, Nature, The New Yorker, Time, GQ, *and* Salon. *In the following viewpoint, Silberman asserts that the use of placebos in medical treatment can be a powerful force of healing, and he contends that patients need not be deceived in order for placebos to work. Placebos, Silberman asserts, are being proven more and more effective, as they consistently outperform medications during clinical drug trials. Silberman presents a study published in 2008 that illustrated how placebos could be used ethically and effectively by informing patients that they could improve their symptoms by simply condi-*

tioning their bodies to tap into their innate healing power through the twice-daily ingestion of a sugar pill. Silberman interviews one of the authors of the 2008 study, Irving Kirsch. Their discussion demonstrates how open placebos might be utilized in regular medical practice, as well as how the placebo effect of antidepressants has increased as the drugs have become more widely prescribed—because people expect the drugs to work, they experience improvements in their symptoms—and how the placebo effect enhances medications, making them much more effective than they would be on their own. Kirsch also contends that the benefits of acupuncture, homeopathy, and other alternative and complementary therapies are almost entirely due to the placebo effect, caused by the time and attention the practitioners give their patients. Kirsch adds that conventional doctors can also elicit a strong placebo effect by spending more time with their patients, listening carefully, and being empathic.

As you read, consider the following questions:

1. What is the Latin origin of the word "placebo," according to Silberman?

2. What kinds of ailments does Kirsch indicate are especially responsive to the placebo effect?

3. What evidence does Kirsch offer to support his contention that it is the act of taking the placebo pill, rather than just the amount of attention that a patient receives from a doctor—what he refers to as the therapeutic relationship—that is responsible for the placebo effect?

A provocative new study called "Placebos Without Deception," published on *PLoS One* today, threatens to make humble sugar pills something they've rarely had a chance to be in the history of medicine: a respectable, ethically sound treatment for disease that has been vetted in controlled trials.

The word *placebo* is ancient, coming to us from the Latin for "I shall please." As far back as the 14th century, the term already had connotations of fakery, sleaze, and deception. For well-to-do Catholic families in Geoffrey Chaucer's day, the custom at funerals was to offer a feast to the congregation after the mourners sang the Office [of] the Dead (which contains the phrase *placebo Domino in regione vivorum*, "I shall please the Lord in the land of the living"). The unintended effect of this largesse [generosity] was to inspire distant relatives and former acquaintances of the departed to crawl out of the woodwork, weeping copiously while praising the deceased, then hastening to the buffet. By the time Chaucer wrote his *The Canterbury Tales*, these macabre freeloaders had been christened "placebo singers."

Placebos Are Complicating the Field of Drug Research

In modern medicine, placebos are associated with another form of deception—a kind that has long been thought essential for conducting randomized clinical trials of new drugs, the statistical rock upon which the global pharmaceutical industry was built. One group of volunteers in an RCT [randomized clinical trial] gets the novel medication; another group (the "control" group) gets pills or capsules that look identical to the allegedly active drug, but contain only an inert substance like milk sugar. These *faux* drugs are called placebos.

Inevitably, the health of some people in both groups improves, while the health of others grows worse. Symptoms of illness fluctuate for all sorts of reasons, including regression to the mean. Since the goal of an RCT, from Big Pharma's [referring to the drug manufacturing industry] perspective, is to demonstrate the effectiveness of a new drug, the return to robust health of a volunteer in the control group is considered a statistical distraction. If too many people in the trial get better after downing sugar pills, the real drug will look worse by comparison—sometimes fatally so for the purpose of earning approval from the Food and Drug Administration.

For a complex and somewhat mysterious set of reasons, it is becoming increasingly difficult for experimental drugs to prove their superiority to sugar pills in RCTs, which was the subject of an in-depth article I published in *Wired* called "The Placebo Problem," recipient of this year's [2010's] AAAS [American Association for the Advancement of Science] Kavli Science Journalism Award for a magazine feature.

Only in recent years, however, has it become obvious that the abatement of symptoms in control-group volunteers—the so-called placebo effect—is worthy of study outside the context of drug trials, and is in fact profoundly good news to anyone but investors in Pfizer, Roche, and GlaxoSmithKline. The emerging field of placebo research has revealed that the body's repertoire of resilience contains a powerful self-healing network that can help reduce pain and inflammation, lower the production of stress chemicals like cortisol, and even tame high blood pressure and the tremors of Parkinson's disease.

Jump-starting this network requires nothing more or less than a belief that one is receiving effective treatment—in the form of a pill, a capsule, talk therapy, injection, IV, or acupuncture needle. The activation of this self-healing network is what we really mean when we talk about the placebo effect. Though inert in themselves, placebos act as passwords between the domain of the mind and the domain of the body, enabling the expectation of healing to be translated into cascades of neurotransmitters and altered patterns of brain activity that engender health.

That's all well and good, but what does it mean in the real world of people getting sick? You can hardly expect the American Medical Association [AMA] to issue a wink and a nod to doctors, encouraging them to prescribe sugar pills for seriously disabling conditions like chronic depression and Parkinson's disease. Meanwhile, more and more studies each year—by researchers like Fabrizio Benedetti at the University of Turin, author of a superb new book called *The Patient's Brain*, and neuroscientist Tor Wager at the University of Colorado [Boulder]—demonstrate that the placebo effect might be potentially useful in treating a wide range of ills. Then why aren't doctors supposed to use it?

The Ethical Dilemma over the Use of Placebos May Be Resolved

The medical establishment's ethical problem with placebo treatment boils down to the notion that for fake drugs to be effective, doctors must lie to their patients. It has been widely assumed that if a patient discovers that he or she is taking a placebo, the mind/body password will no longer unlock the network, and the magic pills will cease to do their job.

Now, however, a group of leading placebo researchers—including Irving Kirsch at the University of Hull in England (who I interview at length below) and Ted Kaptchuk at Harvard—has produced a little bombshell of a study that makes these assumptions obsolete. For "Placebos Without Deception," the researchers tracked the health of 80 volunteers with irritable bowel syndrome [IBS] for three weeks as half of them took placebos and the other half didn't. A painful, chronic gastrointestinal condition, IBS is serious business. It's one of the top ten reasons why people seek medical care worldwide, accounting for millions of dollars a year in health care expenditures and lost work hours.

In a previous study published in the *British Medical Journal* in 2008, Kaptchuk and Kirsch demonstrated that placebo treatment can be highly effective for alleviating the symptoms of IBS. This time, however, instead of the trial being "blinded," it was "open." That is, the volunteers in the placebo group *knew* that they were getting only inert pills—which they were instructed to take religiously, twice a day. They were also informed that, just as Ivan Pavlov trained his dogs to drool at the sound of a bell, the body could be trained to activate its own built-in healing network by the act of swallowing a pill.

In other words, in addition to the bogus medication, the volunteers were given a *true story*—the story of the placebo effect. They also received the care and attention of clinicians, which have been found in many other studies to be crucial for eliciting placebo effects. The combination of the story and a supportive clinical environment were enough to prevail over the knowledge that there was really nothing in the pills. People in the placebo arm of the trial got better—clinically, measurably, significantly better—on standard scales of symptom severity and overall quality of life. In fact, the volunteers in the placebo group experienced improvement comparable to patients taking a drug called Alosetron, the standard of care for IBS.

Meet the ethical placebo: a powerfully effective *faux* medication that meets all the standards of informed consent.

The study is hardly the last word on the subject, but more like one of the first. Its modest sample size and brief duration leave plenty of room for follow-up research. (What if "ethical" placebos wear off more quickly than deceptive ones? Does the fact that most of the volunteers in this study were women have any bearing on the outcome? Were any of the volunteers skeptical that the placebo effect is real, and did that affect their response to treatment?) Before some eager editor out there composes a tweet-baiting headline suggesting that placebos are about to drive Big Pharma out of business, he or she should appreciate the fact that the advent of AMA-approved placebo treatments would open numerous cans of fascinatingly tangled worms. For example, since the precise nature of placebo effects is shaped largely by patients' expectations, would the advertised potency and side effects of theoretical products like Placebex and TheraStim be subject to change by Internet rumors, requiring perpetual updating?

"Placebo" Is No Longer Synonymous with "Ineffective"

Even at this preliminary stage in the research, however, it's clear that it's time to flip our ideas about fake pills upside down. It's common to use the word "placebo" as a synonym for "scam." Economists talk about *placebo solutions* to our economic catastrophe (tax cuts for the rich, anyone?). Online skeptics mock the billion-dollar herbal medicine industry by calling it Big Placebo. The fact that our brains and bodies respond vigorously to placebos given in warm and supportive clinical environments, however, turns out to be very real.

We're also discovering that the *power of narrative* is embedded deeply in our physiology. Perhaps that's not surprising. In the long centuries before doctors discovered antibiotics, they often had little else but an observant eye, a listening ear, and a bag of nostrums with names like decoction of barley and compound infusion of roses to offer their desperately ill patients.

In an age of computerized diagnostics, talking about the power of storytelling in health care seems like a throwback to those medical Dark Ages. After reading the new study, however, one of the pioneers of placebo research, anthropologist Dan Moerman at the University of Michigan, noted how much even the volunteers who didn't get placebos benefited from the support and attention of clinicians.

"I was really surprised at how well the non-placebo group did," Moerman says in an e-mail. "Note I don't call them a 'no treatment group' because they, and everyone else, received exemplary treatment here: They were listened to, examined, encouraged, supported. They were able to talk with, and be taken seriously by, people who understood their issues, things they probably had serious difficulty discussing with their own families. I think it likely that the effectiveness of the placebos above and beyond all the other treatments would have been diminished without the whole system of compassionate care."

At the same time, as Kirsch explains in our interview, the volunteers who took placebos felt significantly better than those who didn't. The act of taking the pills made a difference.

Placebo expert Amir Raz at McGill University observes that the new study follows up on a groundbreaking experiment conducted in 1964 by Lee Park and Uno Covi, who administered "open" placebos to 15 patients from a psychiatric clinic and tracked similar levels of improvement in their anxiety. In a paper slated to be published in the April 2011 issue of the *Canadian Journal of Psychiatry*, Raz will talk to many physicians who doubt that one has to lie to patients for placebos to be effective. In fact, in the real world of doctoring, many physicians prescribe medications at dosages too low to have an effect on their own, hoping to tap into the body's own healing resources—though this is mostly acknowledged only in whispers, as a kind of trade secret.

Kirsch's 2010 book, *The Emperor's New Drugs[: Exploding the Antidepressant Myth]*, caused a huge stir by claiming that the effectiveness of antidepressants—one of the top-selling classes of drugs in the world—may be entirely dependent on the placebo effect. Before spending time with him at a placebo workshop hosted at McGill in July, I was frankly expecting to meet a fiery anti-pharma avenger—albeit one with a compelling argument backed up by data.

Instead, Kirsch is a soft-spoken, modest, diligent, boyishly handsome 67-year-old psychologist who thoroughly understands why his notions are so upsetting to people who insist that their lives have been turned around by Paxil or Lexapro. He also has an intriguing personal history that includes organizing against the Vietnam War with Bertrand Russell, producing a Grammy-nominated comedy album in 1973 with the editors of *National Lampoon*, and playing violin in the Toledo Symphony behind Aretha Franklin. Kirsch is currently working on a new book about the potential of placebo therapy.

The Placebo Effect Can Be a Valuable Treatment Enhancement

Mainstream medicine has tended to dismiss or ignore the placebo effect. Drug companies try to minimize it when conducting clinical trials. But [Harvard Medical School professor Ted] Kaptchuk argues that doctors should instead do everything in their power to try to enhance it by hyping up the rituals around their treatments. Doing so could help make existing treatments more effective and may reduce the need for expensive pills that have lots of side effects. "The ritual of health care has an important role to play that gets overlooked," says Kaptchuk.

Matthew Herper and Robert Langreth,
"The Nothing Cure," Forbes *March 29, 2010.*

Placebo Studies Shed Light on Disease Function and Medication Effectiveness

Silberman: What's the most subversive aspect of this new study?

Kirsch: Simply that placebos work even when you tell people that they're placebos. To me that's fascinating. As is the fact that patients can experience substantial and clinically meaningful improvement of the symptoms of irritable bowel syndrome when given placebos.

One of the assumptions that we made in this study, however, is that you have to offer the patients a convincing rationale to use placebos as well as giving them a pill. That's the next thing we have to test.

What kinds of ailments are amenable to placebo treatment?

Depression, anxiety disorders, and pain; pain in particular is highly responsive to placebo therapy. Irritable bowel syndrome—we've shown that not only in this study, but in one published in the *British Medical Journal* a couple of years ago. Parkinson's disease, ulcers, and asthma, too. There's a long list of conditions treatable with placebos that have some subjective component and can be intensified by conditions like stress.

If all of these ailments have a subjective component, does that mean they share a set of neurological mechanisms?

I'm afraid that's outside my area of expertise. But I know what these conditions *don't* share in common. The kinds of effects you see in the brain when people respond to a placebo depends on the condition you're supposed to be treating. So if you take a placebo analgesic, you get reductions in activity in the brain's pain matrix. If you take a placebo antidepressant, you get changes in brain activity in areas related to depression.

Does the placebo response tell us anything about how active medicines work?

For any condition susceptible to placebos, the placebo effect is a component of the response to active medication. In most cases, placebo effects and drug effects are additive—the net response to the medication is larger because of placebo effects than it would be on its own.

You've done a lot of work analyzing placebo effects in antidepressant therapy, which you write about in your book The Emperor's New Drugs. *Has your opinion of antidepressants evolved at all?*

The more I learn, the more convinced I become that the benefits of drugs for depression are not biologically driven, but driven by the placebo effect. The thing that convinces me most is that nearly all drugs for depression—despite having very different chemical compositions—are of equal benefit. In other words, you have drugs that are completely different in what they do chemically—even drugs that operate by *opposing* mechanisms—creating the same level of effect.

The most commonly employed antidepressants are supposed to increase the amount of serotonin in synapses in the brain, but there are also antidepressants that decrease the level of serotonin in the brain, and they both have the same effect therapeutically. The effects of these drugs seem to be completely independent of their chemical composition.

Dan Moerman mentioned to me in an e-mail that he was surprised by how well the non-placebo group did in your study.

That's true. We said that we compared open label placebo to a no-treatment control group, but actually, the "no-treatment" description is not entirely accurate in this case. The patients in the control group met with the clinician before being given the pills and midway between the beginning and end of the study. Both visits were in the context of a warm, supportive, patient-practitioner relationship. Like many other researchers, we assume that the therapeutic relationship is an important component of the placebo effect.

But many people—including doctors—think that the therapeutic relationship *entirely* accounts for the placebo effect. Our data show that this is not true. If the placebo effect was entirely due to the therapeutic relationship—the time, attention, warmth, and enthusiasm communicated by the doctor—then our placebo pill would not have produced any effect beyond that seen in our "no-treatment" control condition, because the no-treatment control patients received the same level of therapeutic relationship as that received by patients in the placebo-pill condition. That tells us two things—one, that giving patients the placebo pill improved their condition, and two, that the difference in improvement was due to getting the pill. It was not due to the therapeutic relationship.

One of the ways that you prepped the volunteers in this trial was that you informed them that placebo effects work via conditioning, like Pavlov's dogs being trained to salivate at the sound of a bell. What trains people all over the world to respond to the act of taking a pill?

The existence of successful treatments. People come to expect and believe that they're going to get better if they take medication. The whole process of going to a physician and being treated reinforces this belief. That constitutes the basic aspects of classical conditioning. Eventually, the pill alone is enough to produce a placebo effect, whether it contains an active drug or not.

Does direct-to-consumer advertising also play a role? In America, when you open a magazine, the good-looking jock playing with puppies in the sun is the formerly depressed patient on Zoloft.

No doubt about it. One thing that's clear is that the placebo effect of antidepressants has gotten stronger over the years as these drugs have been more widely accepted, touted, and advertised. The response to them in general has increased because of the additivity I was talking about before.

What would a world in which placebos were given openly by doctors look like?

Our study points to something that a number of people have suspected, but has been hard to demonstrate under controlled conditions: We have the capacity for healing physical conditions through psychological means. First, we have to accept that. Studies of placebo effects are great demonstrations of it.

You might think of this healing capacity as a self-regulatory mechanism. Then the question becomes how best to unlock it. This kind of research shows the potential of our being able to treat certain conditions without drugs—particularly in cases where we don't *have* effective drugs, and/or where the drugs we have are not much more effective than what we can accomplish with placebos. And especially in cases where the drugs carry serious risks.

The Placebo Effect Illustrates Benefits of Increased Doctor-Patient Contact

A lot of very smart people dismiss homeopathy, acupuncture, and other alternative treatments as nothing more than quackery for dullards—"woo," as PZ Myers or Ben Goldacre might put it. But couldn't the placebo response play the role of being, in a sense, the "active principle" of woo? For example, I recently saw a controlled trial of homeopathic therapy for rheumatoid arthritis that concluded that the effectiveness of the therapy was due to the homeopathic consultation process, not the little pills themselves. Your colleague Ted Kaptchuk spoke to me for my Wired *article about the importance of "therapeutic ritual" in eliciting the placebo response, and homeopathic consultation—even if the notion that pills containing a few molecules at most of an active ingredient seems obviously ridiculous—is a good example of an elaborate therapeutic ritual. I think the door is still open on whether acupuncture does more than jump-start the placebo response. . . .*

That door is closing. I think the effects of acupuncture are largely placebo effects, if not entirely. It's a very *good* placebo effect; a really healthy and large placebo effect. The last study we did on IBS was with placebo acupuncture—sham acupuncture. Sham acupuncture does as much good as real acupuncture. You can do it without needles and still get the same effect. Practitioners of acupuncture, homeopathy, and other alternative and complementary medicines do an excellent job of eliciting and bolstering placebo effects.

We know from our research the things that make a difference: how much time you spend with a patient, how supportive and empathic you are, how well you listen, and how confident you are in being able to help. Complementary and alternative medicine practitioners are particularly good at these things. These are obviously things that physicians can do as well, and some are very good at eliciting placebo effects.

But those qualities are becoming more rare in conventional medical practice. Certainly here in the UK [United Kingdom], it's very uncommon to have a good placebo intervention in primary care, because the standard visit with the doctor is ten minutes at most.

Ten minutes sounds long to me. If I see my doctor for three minutes as she rushes around, it's a good day.

In the IBS study we did in 2008, we maximized the amount of time spent in the initial interview, and other qualities of listening and empathy, and got much more substantial placebo effects.

"If the substance is viewed as helpful, it can heal, but if it is viewed as harmful, it can cause negative effects."

Placebo Treatment Can Have Harmful as Well as Beneficial Effects

Eliezer Sobel

Eliezer Sobel is a journalist who has contributed articles to several periodicals including Tikkun, Yoga Journal, Village Voice, Mudfish, *and* Quest Magazine. *He was the publisher and editor of the* Wild Heart Journal *and is the author of the book* The 99th Monkey: A Spiritual Journalist's Misadventures with Gurus, Messiahs, Sex, Psychedelics, and Other Consciousness-Raising Experiments. *In the following viewpoint, Sobel argues that the benefits of antidepressant medications may have more to do with the placebo effect than the efficacy of the drugs themselves. Sobel points to the fact that companies had to conduct several trials for some antidepressants in order to get two positive results, which is the minimum required for approval by the US Food and Drug Administration (FDA). The negative results were never published, Sobel argues, and the positive results showed only marginally greater benefits over placebos. This, Sobel explains, furthered the reputation of antidepressant medications as effective treatments, which then enhanced the placebo effect experienced by drug trial participants who figured out that they were taking an actual medication versus a placebo because of the side effects that they experienced. This placebo effect is legitimate and helpful, Sobel concludes, but he cautions that patients can also experience withdrawal symptoms and a "nocebo" effect, which is the impact of the brain's response to what it perceives as a harmful substance or event.*

As you read, consider the following questions:

1. For what medication does Sobel say he was given a $90 refund by the Bristol-Myers company, and what side effect does he say that he experienced as a result of taking this medication?

2. How many clinical trials did the makers of Prozac have to run before they were able to produce the minimum two positive results required for FDA approval, according to Sobel?

3. What is the term used to describe the principle behind the phenomenon of the brain's ability to respond accordingly based on whether it perceives a stimulus as positive or negative, according to Sobel?

It could be argued that Wikipedia is not the most scholarly or accurate resource for medical information. On the other hand, I am not a physician or a psychologist, so please cut me some slack.

From Wikipedia: "The patient is given an inert pill, told that it may improve his/her condition, but not told that it is in fact inert. Such an intervention may cause the patient to believe the treatment will change his/her condition; and this belief may produce a subjective perception of a therapeutic effect, causing the patient to feel their condition has improved. This phenomenon is known as the *placebo effect*."

My first foray into the nebulous world of antidepressants was in 1985 when I was put on Sinequan. It gave me severe cotton mouth, didn't do much for my mood, but came with the side benefit of causing rather compelling lucid dreams immediately upon falling asleep every night, which I rather enjoyed. In the quarter century since then, I've experimented, for periods ranging from one night to one year, with Prozac, Zoloft (a one-nighter; it gave me the jumping-out-of-my-skin heebie-jeebies, as did Effexor and Trazodone), Paxil, Serzone (I received a $90 refund from Bristol-Myers when a refill caused six hours of vomiting and a call to Poison Control), Neurontin (stopped after two days when talking to the assistant headmaster at my school and noticed that my consciousness seemed to be about two feet behind and slightly above my voice which appeared to be emerging from the area in and around my mouth), Wellbutrin, Buspar, Lamictal (again, only for two days, until I finished reading all the potential side effects including the ominous black-box death warning on the package, and worse, mention of an incurable rash), Seroquel (one night only, got up to pee, stepped on and broke the cat's water bowl and smashed my head into a floor lamp; when I reported this to my psychiatrist, he said, "Oh, I forgot to mention that that's one of the side effects of Seroquel, except people usually end up banging their head on the bathroom floor."), Abilify, Adderall, and Xanax, Klonopin and/or Valium to take the edge off, Ambien for sleep, and marijuana for energy. (I often had what my doctor called "paradoxical reactions" to medications, meaning, for example, that whereas for many people marijuana is a lethargy-inducing occasion to eat Ring-Dings and watch endless reruns of *Mr. Ed* on Nickelodeon, in my case, one or two tokes and I'd be off on a 20-mile bike ride.)

Doctors Should Focus on Attitude and Enthusiasm and Not on Placebos

The uses of placebos simply cannot coexist with our health care's principles of autonomy and informed consent.... The development of good rapport with patients through honesty and openness may activate patient responses similar to the placebo effect. Finally, as studies of placebos show, the belief of physicians in their prescribed therapy can increase positive outcomes by 40%. Thus, physicians should show sincere enthusiasm and recommend only the best evidence-based therapies for their patients.

Jason Wong,
"Ethical Considerations of Placebo Treatment,"
University of Alberta Health Sciences Journal, *vol. 3, no. 1,*
June 2006.

Published Studies Have Downplayed the Placebo Effect

Thus, it was with great interest that I read Irving Kirsch's recent book, *The Emperor's New Drugs: Exploding the Antidepressant Myth*. Kirsch makes a compelling, carefully researched, scientific case for the fact that nearly all of the benefits reported by users of antidepressants are a result of the placebo effect. *Note to satisfied users,* and I count myself among them, at least sometimes: This does *not* mean that the results and benefits you experience from these drugs are not real or true; nobody is invalidating the truth of your direct experience.

What Kirsch *does* explain, however, is that there have been literally thousands and thousands of studies of antidepressants conducted by the big pharmaceutical companies that revealed *no significant results whatsoever*; however, they generally opted *not* to publish those particular studies, thus making them unavailable to both the public and to *your psychiatrist*! Kirsch invoked the Freedom of Information Act to demand the release of the studies by the FDA [US Food and Drug Administration] for his perusal. So that's point number one. Taken. (Buy the book for your shrink!)

"Companies have had to conduct numerous trials to get two that show a positive result, which is the Food and Drug Administration's minimum for approval. The makers of Prozac had to run five trials to obtain two that were positive, and the makers of Paxil and Zoloft had to run even more." (From "Against Depression, a Sugar Pill Is Hard to Beat," *Washington Post*, May 7, 2002.)

Worse: The studies that *were* published and released mostly revealed only negligible and "barely significant" positive results and benefits over placebos in double-blind experiments. Worse yet: Kirsch demonstrates, again with compelling arguments, that even those slightly beneficial results were *themselves* the result of the placebo effect, for this reason: In a double-blind study, neither the subjects nor the researchers are aware of who is receiving what. However, those receiving the actual medication would soon start to experience their all-too-real side effects, and thus would conclude early on that they indeed were the lucky ones and the positive benefits of the placebo effect would immediately kick in.

Yes, he's saying that the slight advantage of antidepressants over placebos are the result of the placebo effect.

It's placebo over placebo, by a nose.

The Placebo Effect Can Be Harmful

But don't knock the placebo effect; it has been demonstrated to not only have countless positive health benefits in unsuspecting patients, it can also produce withdrawal symptoms when discontinued, or, when used in the opposite manner, can produce the "nocebo" effect; that is, cause harm. A placebo described as a muscle relaxant will cause muscle *relaxation*, but if the identical substance is presented as the opposite, muscle *tension* will result. A placebo presented as a stimulant will *raise* heart rhythm and blood pressure, but when administered as a depressant, it will *lower* both.

The principle behind this phenomenon has been termed "the meaning response," referring to the brain's power to generate effects in response to whatever it believes to be true, positive or negative. If the substance is viewed as helpful, it can heal, but if it is viewed as harmful, it can cause negative effects. Because the placebo effect is based upon expectations and conditioning, when a subject who has benefited from a placebo is later informed that they had in fact *not* received the genuine medication, their condition would often rapidly deteriorate and the positive placebo effects would disappear.

Even when an inert substance is producing positive, healing results in people, the recipients can nullify the intended placebo effect simply by having a negative attitude toward its effectiveness, often quickly transforming the same substance into a harmful nocebo. One researcher even coined a term for this situation: "the placebo paradox." It states that, "While it may be unethical to use a placebo, it may also be unethical *not* to [use one]." (Dr. David Newman, author of *Hippocrates' Shadow: Secrets from the House of Medicine—What Doctors Don't Know, Don't Tell You, and How Truth Can Repair the Patient-Doctor Breach*)

When I read Kirsch's book and became convinced of his point of view, I had already been feeling dissatisfied with my latest antidepressant cocktail anyway, so I opted to wean myself once again, for the umpteenth time in as many years (umpteen), armed with the knowledge that my paltry mood improvements were both minimal *and* placebo induced, and not worth the principle side effect for me, which is insomnia. The price I'm paying, however, is the loss of those "barely significant" results that I *did* receive when I was still a believer, and as a result, last night I had a dream in which I was sobbing, and I woke up in literal tears. My brother, a psychologist, appeared in the dream just before I regained consciousness, to say, "Be careful; the placebo effect can kill you."

Periodical and Internet Sources Bibliography

The following articles have been selected to supplement the diverse views presented in this chapter.

Meredith Cohn	"Cancer Patients Turn to Acupuncture to Cope with Symptoms, Side Effects," *Baltimore Sun*, September 30, 2011.
Joseph Mosquera	"Doctors, Patients Are Conflicted About Alternative Medicine," *Consumer Reports*, September 28, 2011.
Eric Nelson	"Medicine That's Truly Complementary," *Blogcritics*, October 14, 2011. http://blog critics.org.
Anahad O'Connor	"The Doctor's Remedy: Turmeric for Joint Pain," *Well Blog: Tara Parker-Pope on Health*, October 19, 2011. http://well.blogs.nytimes .com.
Orac	"Alternative Medicine: The Illusion of Control," *Respectful Insolence*, October 17, 2011. http:// scienceblogs.com.
Kevin B. O'Reilly	"Demand Drives More Hospitals to Offer Alternative Therapies," Amednews.com, October 4, 2011. www.ama-assn.org.
Susan Pugh	"Looking at the Whole Picture: Integrative Medicine Offers Partnership between Doctor and Patient for Healing," *News & Advance* (Lynchburg, PA), October 16, 2011.
Jon C. Tilburt and Kimball C. Atwood IV	"Open Communication Valuable in Weighing Alternative Medicine Requests," Amednews .com, October 10, 2011. www.ama-assn.org.

OPPOSING VIEWPOINTS® SERIES

How Should Government Research and Regulate Alternative Medicine?

Chapter Preface

On October 18, 2011, the US Food and Drug Administration (FDA) issued the following public notification on its website: "FDA laboratory analysis confirmed that 'Ja Dera 100% Natural Weight Loss Supplement' contains sibutramine. Sibutramine is a controlled substance that was removed from the U.S. market in October 2010 for safety reasons. The product poses a threat to consumers because sibutramine is known to substantially increase blood pressure and/or pulse rate in some patients and may present a significant risk for patients with a history of coronary artery disease, congestive heart failure, arrhythmias, or stroke. This product may also interact in life-threatening ways with other medications a consumer may be taking."[1] The FDA adds: "This notification is to inform the public of a growing trend of products marketed as dietary supplements or conventional foods with hidden drugs and chemicals. These products are typically promoted for sexual enhancement, weight loss, and body building, and are often represented as being 'all natural.'" According to an August 27, 2011, *New York Times* article by Natasha Singer, US Customs Service officers at New York City's Kennedy airport recently began using a new device to detect the presence of pharmaceuticals in shipments of supplements. Singer reports: "Since this facility began using the device this year, it has detected the drug [sibutramine] in 35 out of 36 packages of weight-loss products."[2] At the FDA laboratory in Philadelphia, Singer adds, testing reveals that one brand of diet pills contains "more than 30 milligrams [of sibutramine] per unit—or roughly six times more than the starting dose of the legal medicine when it was on the market."

Steve Mister, president and CEO of the Council for Responsible Nutrition, a leading dietary supplement industry trade group, issued a statement in support of the FDA's efforts in December 2010, when the FDA issued a letter to supplement manufacturers, asking them for their assistance in combating the problem of drug-tainted dietary supplements. Mister makes it clear that the industry supports government efforts to curb illegal activity, but he points out that the majority of supplement manufacturers operate safe, legal facilities, and that only a few rogue manufacturers are to blame for the tainted products. Mister asserts: "Although our companies are not part of the problem, we want to be part of the solution."[3] Singer reports that Mister comments that the industry has decided to focus on maintaining their own safeguards rather than on notifying the public of potential hazards posed by supplements produced by illegitimate outfits, because, Mister notes, "We are concerned that if we alert consumers, we may unnecessarily drive them away from the marketplace. We could make them afraid to take legitimate dietary supplements." Singer also interviewed Mister for a February 9, 2009, *New York Times* article covering the recall of StarCaps, a popular brand of weight-loss supplement. Mister, Singer reports, "said that the majority of weight-loss supplements were safe," but, she adds, "a half-dozen experts interviewed for this article, including government scientists, health activists, doctors and a professor of pharmacy, said that even mainstream natural weight-loss supplements that did not contain hidden drugs could be risky. And they questioned whether such supplements could have any significant effect on weight."[4]

The debate over the regulation and safety of dietary supplements is closely examined in this chapter of *Opposing Viewpoints: Alternative Medicine*. The viewpoints in this chapter also focus on the funding and purpose of the National Center for Complementary and Alternative Medicine as well as on the concerns over consumer freedom, public health hazards, and the economic viability of the American dietary supplement industry relating to proposed legislation to increase the US government's regulatory control over the labeling, manufacturing, and marketing of dietary supplements.

Notes

1. US Food and Drug Administration, "Public Notification: 'Ja Dera 100% Natural Weight Loss Supplement' Contains Undeclared Drug Ingredient," October 18, 2011. www.fda.gov.
2. Natasha Singer, "Ingredients of Shady Origins, Posing as Supplements," *New York Times*, August 27, 2011.
3. Steve Mister, "Comments Delivered by Steve Mister, President & CEO Council for Responsible Nutrition at the Food and Drug Administration Teleconference, December 15, 2010," Council for Responsible Nutrition, www.crnusa.org.
4. Natasha Singer, "F.D.A. Finds 'Natural' Diet Pills Laced with Drugs," *New York Times*, February 9, 2009.

> "Results from NCCAM-supported research will enable evidence-based decision making by the general public, health care professionals, and health policy makers about CAM use."

The National Center for Complementary and Alternative Medicine Should Be Funded

National Center for Complementary and Alternative Medicine

The National Center for Complementary and Alternative Medicine (NCCAM) is an agency within the National Institutes of Health that is dedicated to conducting scientific research on complementary and alternative medicine (CAM) to help inform decisions surrounding the use of such treatments to promote health and well-being. In the following viewpoint, NCCAM outlines its justification for continued government funding, highlighting the importance of its role in improving health care for all Americans. *The agency asserts that there is a great need for reliable and objective scientific research on alternative treatments, most of which have never been subjected to formal clinical trials, in order to protect the public against treatments that may be harmful or that make fraudulent claims about their effectiveness. The viewpoint highlights NCCAM programs that are studying the potential medical applications of botanicals and mindfulness meditation. These and other research programs, the agency contends, are using specific research models and techniques that will ensure that the positive results can be quickly translated into new, widely available medical treatments.*

As you read, consider the following questions:

1. What year was the NCCAM established, according to the viewpoint?

2. For what type of symptoms experienced by women do two of the Botanical Research Centers hope to find effective treatments, according to the viewpoint?

3. How is "neuroplasticity" defined in the viewpoint, and what is its significance?

The National Center for Complementary and Alternative Medicine (NCCAM) is the federal government's lead agency for scientific research on complementary and alternative medicine (CAM). NCCAM's mission is to define, through rigorous scientific investigation, the usefulness and safety of complementary and alternative medicine interventions and their role in improving health and health care. CAM is a group of diverse health-related disciplines, practices, and products that are not generally considered to be part of conventional medicine. Scientific evidence from NCCAM-supported research informs decision making by the public, by health care professionals, and by health policy makers regarding the use of CAM interventions and their integration into strategies for better health care and promoting health.

CAM is used by many in the United States to treat health problems and promote better health. Data from National Health Interview Surveys, developed under NCCAM leadership and conducted by the National Center for Health Statistics at the Centers for Disease Control and Prevention (CDC), show that nearly 40 percent of adult Americans and 12 percent of children are using some form of CAM. These data also show that Americans spent $33.9 billion out of pocket for CAM in 2007. This amount accounted for approximately 1.5 percent of total health care expenditures, but more than 11 percent of total out-of-pocket health care expenditures. The data also suggest that CAM use is very often for self-care, i.e., not under the advice or supervision of a health professional.

Identifying Future CAM Research Priorities

Building on more than 10 years of progress, NCCAM is focusing its research efforts on specific areas of scientific promise. For example, research suggests that acupuncture may provide relief for chronic pain such as low-back pain and osteoarthritis of the knee. Established in 1999, NCCAM is shaping its future through its third strategic plan, developed with input from its diverse stakeholder community. The strategic plan is built around three long-range goals aimed at improving the state and use of scientific evidence regarding the two major reasons for use of CAM in the United States—treating health problems and supporting or promoting better health and well-being. The three goals are to: (1) advance the science and practice of symptom management; (2) develop effective, practical, personalized strategies for promoting health and well-being; and (3) enable better evidence-based decision making regarding CAM use and its integration into health care and health promotion.

(1) Advancing the Science and Practice of Symptom Management

Emerging scientific evidence suggests that some CAM approaches—such as massage, acupuncture, spinal manipulation, and meditation—may be helpful in managing symptoms such as chronic back or neck pain, or pain from arthritis or other musculoskeletal problems. For example, recent research suggests that people with fibromyalgia may benefit from practicing tai chi, which combines meditation, slow movements, deep breathing and relaxation. Other studies suggest that these interventions may engage innate biological processes involved in pain and emotion. NCCAM plans to support research that aims to elucidate more clearly how such promising CAM interventions could add value to existing health care approaches. This research will include the study of the safety of CAM interventions and identifying the mechanisms by which they exert biological effects.

(2) Developing Effective and Practical Strategies for Promoting Health and Well-Being

Research has shown that sustaining or improving healthy behaviors (such as good eating habits and regular exercise) and reducing or eliminating unhealthy behaviors (such as smoking) can reduce an individual's risk of chronic disease. Many CAM or integrative medicine practitioners encourage use of meditative and other mind/body approaches to help motivate people to adopt and sustain health-seeking behaviors. These approaches may include physical activities like yoga and healthy eating practices that may be grounded in traditional medical systems or incorporate a healthy food philosophy. Emerging evidence suggests that CAM use may be associated with greater degrees of health-seeking behavior. While causal relationships between CAM use and healthy behavior have not been established, the claims and preliminary data deserve investigation given the formidable public health challenges in motivating behavior change. NCCAM plans to sponsor research exploring whether CAM-inclusive approaches are useful in encouraging improved self-care and greater commitment to a healthy lifestyle.

(3) Enabling Evidence-Based Decision Making Regarding Use and Integration of CAM

The public, health professionals, and policy makers need reliable, objective, evidence-based information regarding CAM. Providing such information so that they can make informed decisions about CAM use is of paramount importance to NCCAM, and central to the center's successful fulfillment of its legislative mandate. Importantly, evidence from several sources suggests that CAM research findings do influence CAM use by the public. NCCAM will continue to use state-of-the-art technologies and approaches to improve access to evidence-based information on CAM for the general public and health professionals.

A decade of investment in research on a broad array of CAM modalities indicates that some approaches may lead to improved strategies for treating bothersome symptoms or promoting better health. Building on this foundation, NCCAM will continue funding rigorous scientific investigations to advance the body of evidence regarding the safety and efficacy of CAM interventions. Such evidence is also essential to efforts to integrate CAM interventions of proven safety and efficacy into health care and disease prevention strategies. Results from NCCAM-supported research will enable evidence-based decision making by the general public, health care professionals, and health policy makers about CAM use. . . .

Program Descriptions and Accomplishments

Extramural Basic Research. Basic research clarifies fundamental biological effects that are central to the development of the evidence base in complementary and alternative medicine and underpins the design of clinical research. NCCAM supports investigator-initiated basic research and will increase, through targeted initiatives, its support for translational research [a type of research that focuses on quickly translating study re-

Senator Tom Harkin on Government Support for Alternative Medicine

It is time to end the discrimination against alternative health care practices. . . .

And it is time to adopt an integrative approach that takes advantage of the very best scientifically based medicines and therapies, whether conventional or alternative.

This is about giving people the pragmatic alternatives they want, while ending discrimination against practitioners of scientifically based alternative health care. It is about improving health care outcomes. And, yes, it is about reducing health care costs. Generally speaking, alternative therapies are less expensive and less intrusive— and we need to take advantage of that. . . .

In 1992, at my urging, Congress passed legislation creating the Office of Alternative Medicine at the National Institutes of Health. In 1998, I sponsored legislation to elevate that office to what, today, is the National Center for Complementary and Alternative Medicine. That center is sponsoring extraordinarily important research. . . .

Today, we are not just talking about alternative practices but also the integration between conventional and alternative therapies in order to achieve truly integrative health. We need to have practitioners talking with each other, collaborating to treat the whole person. . . .

If we fail to seize this unique opportunity to adopt a pragmatic, integrative approach to health care, then that, too, would constitute a serious failure.

Tom Harkin, "Statement by Senator Tom Harkin at the Hearing on the Use of Integrative Care to Keep People Healthy," Tom Harkin, Iowa's Senator: Blog, *February 26, 2009. http://harkin.senate.gov.*

sults into practical medical applications] on promising CAM interventions. NCCAM funds basic research initiatives such as "Mechanistic Research on CAM Natural Products," which will support development of advanced technologies and methodologies to study natural products. Knowledge of the active components as well as the biological effects of natural products is critical for designing clinical studies to determine the efficacy of these products.

Budget Policy: The FY [fiscal year] 2012 NCCAM budget estimate for extramural basic research is $47.6 million, an increase of $864 thousand or 1.8 percent above the FY 2010 enacted level. The FY 2012 basic research plan supports an increase of the evidence base on the physiological mechanisms underlying CAM practices as well as the development and validation of methods and approaches needed to ensure that clinical research has a solid foundation and facilitates the integration of proven CAM approaches into health care. The program portrait listed below describes the Botanical Research Centers program.

Botanical Research Centers Enable Evidence-Based Decision Making on Natural Product Use.

FY 2010 $3.2 million

FY 2012 $3.2 million

Although the safety and efficacy of many botanical dietary supplements have not been adequately studied, they are still widely used throughout the United States. To advance understanding of how botanicals may affect human health, NIH [National Institutes of Health] is finding five interdisciplinary and collaborative dietary supplement centers that are known as the Botanical Research Centers (BRC) program. The BRCs will conduct studies of the safety, efficacy, and biological action of botanical supplements and conduct research with a high potential of being translated into practical strategies to benefit human health.

This program is intended to advance the science of botanical research, from careful identification of constituents of botanicals to early phase clinical studies of safety and efficacy. Preclinical research that will inform future clinical studies is encouraged as the primary research focus of this program. Many of the BRCs are employing high-throughput technologies [automating experiments to make them easier to conduct on a large scale] to advance understanding of the biological effects of natural products and define their mechanisms of action, or how they work in the human body.

Two of the BRCs are researching botanicals that may show promise for reducing the troublesome menopausal symptoms experienced by nearly two-thirds of perimenopausal women. One BRC is focusing on the safety of botanical dietary supplements that are widely available and used by women (e.g., black cohosh, licorice) to determine biological effects and explore possible interactions with prescription drugs. Another BRC is studying botanical products that contain estrogen-like compounds, called phytoestrogens, to determine their safety, efficacy, and mechanism of action.

The BRCs are located at the Pennington Biomedical Research Center, Baton Rouge, Louisiana; University of Illinois at Chicago; University of Illinois at Urbana-Champaign; University of Missouri, Columbia; and Wake Forest University Health Sciences, Winston-Salem, North Carolina. They are jointly funded by NCCAM and the NIH Office of Dietary Supplements. Additionally, the National Cancer Institute is co-supporting two of the five centers.

Extramural Clinical Research. The NCCAM extramural research program funds multidisciplinary clinical investigations into various CAM modalities at leading U.S. biomedical and CAM research institutions. Clinical CAM research ranges from small pilot studies to large-scale clinical trials and epidemiological studies [studies that focus on finding or testing cause and effect relationships, e.g., smoking and lung cancer] supported through solicited research initiatives, collaboration between NIH institutes and centers and the CDC, and investigator-initiated research. As part of this effort, NCCAM will explore the use of outcomes and effectiveness research in developing practice-based evidence on how CAM approaches could aid in better symptom management and thereby help to reduce the public health burden of chronic diseases and troublesome conditions. The benefits of this research are two-fold: It will help to inform our understanding of CAM use as practiced in the community, and it will provide additional data on the effectiveness of CAM interventions for particular diseases and symptoms.

Budget Policy: The FY 2012 NCCAM budget estimate for extramural clinical research is $48.2 million, an increase of $963 thousand or 2.0 percent above the FY 2010 enacted level. The NCCAM extramural clinical research plan will target the strategic priorities of support for CAM efficacy and effectiveness research, with the ultimate goal to inform the scientific evidence base on CAM for specific indications. The program portrait listed below provides an overview of NCCAM's meditative practices program.

Understanding How Emotional Responses Can Be Regulated by Meditative Practices.

FY 2010 $14.3 million

FY 2012 $14.5 million

Meditation may be practiced for many reasons, including possible health benefits such as increased calmness and physical relaxation, improved coping with stress or illness, or enhanced overall health and well-being. Meditative practices include meditation as well as other mind-body practices that incorporate movement with meditation such as yoga and tai chi. Clinical and laboratory studies of mindfulness meditation are yielding a growing body of evidence that meditation affects the mind, the brain, the body, and behavior in ways that have promise for treatment of many health problems, and for promoting healthy behavior.

Research suggests that systematic mindfulness training and other meditation practices influence areas of the brain involved in regulating awareness, attention, and emotion. Brain imaging studies suggest that more mindful people may be better able to regulate emotional reactions or have improved self-awareness. Other research suggests that mental training causes structural changes in the brain through the processes of neuroplasticity (the ability of the brain to change as a result of one's experiences). Several studies suggest that meditative practices can positively affect immune function. Many of the beneficial physical effects of mindfulness training could be attributable to learning to cope better with stress.

Investigators are studying the use of mindfulness training in treating specific pain conditions, overeating and obesity, irritable bowel syndrome, insomnia, myocardial ischemia (or angina), and substance abuse. Specifically, NCCAM is supporting studies investigating meditation for: diminishing symptoms of chronic back pain, improving attention-related abilities (focusing and prioritizing), relieving stress in caregivers for elderly patients with dementia, alleviating asthma symptoms, and reducing the frequency and intensity of hot flashes in menopausal women. Mindfulness mediation is also being explored as a means of facilitating and sustaining healthy behavior change, for example smoking cessation or healthier eating habits.

Extramural Research Training and Capacity Building. The basic, translational, and clinical research required to develop the evidence base for CAM is enhanced through the expertise of CAM practitioners working in partnership with conventional researchers. To increase the number, quality, and diversity of investigators who conduct research on CAM, NCCAM supports a variety of training and career development activities for predoctoral and postdoctoral students, CAM practitioners, and conventional medical researchers and practitioners. For example, NCCAM supports programs aimed at enhancing CAM practitioners' abilities to evaluate biomedical literature, participate in clinical research, and seek advanced training and career development opportunities. Researchers from many different biomedical and behavioral disciplines have the expertise required for in-depth investigation of the basic biological, physiological, and clinical effects and safety of CAM interventions; therefore, NCCAM supports programs to attract these researchers to CAM research and partnerships with CAM practitioners.

Budget Policy: The NCCAM FY 2012 budget proposal for extramural research training and capacity building is $11.5 million, an increase of $0.182 million or 1.6 percent above the FY 2010 enacted level. To address the ongoing need to build and sustain CAM research capacity, NCCAM will make awards under its ongoing training initiatives that target CAM and conventional investigators at various stages of their careers, including Ruth L. Kirschstein National Research Service Awards, Mentored Patient-Oriented Research Career Development Award, and Midcareer Investigator Award in Patient-Oriented Research. NIH will provide an across-the-board increase in FY 2012 of four percent for stipend levels under the Ruth L. Kirschstein National Research Service Award training program to continue efforts to attain the stipend levels recommended by the National Academy of Sciences. This will build on the two percent increase in stipend levels for FY 2011. Stipend levels have lagged significantly behind inflation, and increases are necessary to sustain the development of a highly qualified biomedical research workforce.

Intramural Research. NCCAM is partnering with other NIH institutes and centers to develop innovative investigations that will expand intramural interdisciplinary research collaborations in areas such as neuroscience and neuroimaging. Research supported under this program will focus on ways that different CAM modalities (e.g., acupuncture) modulate pain and other symptoms.

Budget Policy: The FY 2012 NCCAM budget proposal for intramural research is $8.2 million, an increase of $80 thousand or 1.0 percent above the FY 2010 enacted level.

Research Management and Support (RMS). Through its RMS activities, including grants review and management, NCCAM continues to fund meritorious basic, clinical, and translational research and research training efforts. NCCAM is also providing important trans-NIH leadership on the significant public health problem of back pain, for example, through workshops aimed at defining a research agenda, or on scientific issues regarding control/comparison groups for trials of non-pharmacologic interventions. Additionally, the center continues to provide reliable, objective, and evidence-based information to help the public make informed decisions about CAM use and to enable health care providers to better manage their patients' care. For example, the Time To Talk outreach initiative encourages patients and their health care providers to discuss CAM use.

Budget Policy: The FY 2012 NCCAM budget proposal for research management and support is $15.5 million, an increase of $146 thousand or 1.0 percent above the FY 2010 enacted level.

> "Scarce NIH funds should not be for projects that have as their basis hypotheses that are outlandishly implausible from a scientific standpoint."

The National Center for Complementary and Alternative Medicine Should Not Be Funded

David Gorski

David Gorski is a surgical oncologist and the American College of Surgeons' Commission on Cancer liaison physician at the Barbara Ann Karmanos Cancer Institute in Detroit, Michigan; he is also an associate professor of surgery at Wayne State University, also in Detroit. In the following viewpoint, Gorski argues that the National Center for Complementary and Alternative Medicine (NCCAM) is a complete waste of American taxpayer dollars because, he maintains, the agency promotes alternative and complementary therapies in the absence of, and at the expense of, rigorous scientific evidence that they are effective. Gorski il-

David Gorski, "The National Center for Complementary and Alternative Medicine (NCCAM): Your Tax Dollars Hard at Work," Science-Based Medicine, February 4, 2008. www.sciencebasedmedicine.org. Copyright © 2008 by Science-Based Medicine. All rights reserved. Reproduced by permission.

lustrates that the vast majority of research grants funded by the NCCAM are used to study therapies that have demonstrated little or no concrete evidence that they are beneficial, or to study herbal remedies, which could be studied under the auspices of any number of other agencies within the National Institutes of Health (NIH). Gorski points out that because the NCCAM was founded by influential lawmakers who are proponents of alternative medicine and because its advisory board is required to be staffed by alternative medicine practitioners and leading representatives of alternative and complementary medicine, the studies approved by funding are unlikely to be those that threaten to disprove the validity of the very treatment systems that make up the source of income for the agency's leadership. The agency is not interested in determining which remedies work, Gorski asserts, but merely wishes to lend credibility to bogus complementary and alternative therapies for financial gain.

As you read, consider the following questions:

1. How many grants are awarded to study herbs, supplements, and dietary interventions, according to the viewpoint?

2. How many grants for fellowships or large collaborative CAM centers or projects does NCCAM fund, according to Gorski?

3. What type of alternative medicine does Gorski identify as the most scientifically implausible?

What's an advocate of evidence- and science-based medicine to think about the National Center for Complementary and Alternative Medicine, better known by its abbreviation NCCAM? As I've pointed out before, I used to be somewhat of a supporter of NCCAM. I really did, back when I was more naïve and idealistic. Indeed, as I mentioned before, when I first read Wally Sampson's article "Why NCCAM should be defunded," I thought it a bit too strident and even rather close-minded. At the time, I thought that the best way to separate the wheat from the chaff was to apply the scientific method to the various "CAM [complementary and alternative medicine]" modalities and let the chips fall where they may.

Two developments over the last several years have led me to sour on NCCAM and move towards an opinion more like Dr. Sampson's. First, after its doubling from FY [fiscal year] 1998–2003, the NIH [National Institutes of Health] budget stopped growing. In fact, adjusting for inflation, the NIH budget is now contracting. NCCAM's yearly budget remains in the range of $121 million a year, for well over $1 billion spent since its inception as the Office of Alternative Medicine in 1993. Its yearly budget contains enough money to fund around 75 to 100 new five-year R01 grants [a highly sought after type of NIH grant], give or take. In tight budgetary times my view is that it is a grossly irresponsible use of taxpayer money not to prioritize funding for projects that have hypotheses behind them that have a reasonable chance of being true. Scarce NIH funds should not be for projects that have as their basis hypotheses that are outlandishly implausible from a scientific standpoint. Second, I've seen over the last few years how NCCAM is not only funding research (most of which is of the sort that wouldn't stand a chance in a study section from other institutes or centers) but it's funding training programs. Indeed, that was the core complaint against NCCAM: that it facilitates and promotes the infiltration of nonscience- and nonevidence-based treatments falling under the rubric of so-called "complementary and alternative" or "integrative" medicine into academic medicine. However, NCCAM cannot do otherwise, given its mission:

- Explore complementary and alternative healing practices in the context of rigorous science.

- Train complementary and alternative medicine researchers.

- Disseminate authoritative information to the public and professionals.

If, in fact, NCCAM actually did devote itself solely to "rigorous science" with regard to "alternative" healing practices, I would have much less problem with it than I do. However, it broadly interprets the second and third parts of its mission. For example, it views part of its mission as promotion, rather than study: "Supporting integration of proven CAM therapies. Our research helps the public and health professionals understand which CAM therapies have been proven to be safe and effective." This would be all well and good if NCCAM had as yet actually proven any CAM therapies to be at least effective, but it has not. Worse, it has not even managed to demonstrate any of them to be *ineffective*, either, thus leading to endless studies of modalities that either do not work or at the very least would have marginal efficacy.

Still, I thought, all questions of promotion of CAM modalities aside, at least there's the science. Surely, under the auspices of the NIH, NCCAM must be funding some high-quality studies into CAM modalities that couldn't be done any other way. That thought died when NCCAM announced last week [in February 2008] the studies that it had funded during FY 2007.

Types of Grants Funded by the NIH

Before I discuss the studies, it's useful to explain briefly for the benefit of those not familiar with NIH grant mechanisms (in other words, the vast majority of our readers) just exactly what the alphabet-number soup describing the types of NIH grants means:

- *R01.* The gold standard of NIH research awards, this mechanism describes investigator-initiated multiyear grants (usually four or five years) to study whatever the investigator wants to study, provided that he or she can convince a study section of the worth of the project and that the project is related to the program interests of one of the NIH institutes. As such, they generally require a fairly large amount of preliminary data and a well-defined research plan to study a clear and scientifically reasonable and interesting hypothesis.

- *R21.* These grants are usually one- or two-year exploratory rewards designed to investigate more risky hypotheses. As such, they require much less, if any, preliminary data.

- *P01 and P50.* P series awards are known as program project grants and are intended to fund large, multi-investigator projects (P01), often encompassing more than one institution, or research center (P50).

- *K awards.* These awards are intended to fund the development of junior faculty and are also known as career development awards. The idea is that these awards, which require a mentor to support and guide the applicant, are supposed to be a bridge to independent funding.

- *Small Business Research Awards (R41, R42, R43, R44).* These are granted to small businesses to fund the development of (usually) biotech and related projects.

- *T32.* T32 and related grants fund training and fellowship programs. For example, my surgical oncology fellowship was funded by a T32 award, and our cancer institute has a T32 to fund medical oncology fellows who want to spend two years in the lab.

Figure 1. NIH Funding Mechanisms

Award mechanism	Number of NCCAM grants funded in FY2007
P01/P50	18
R01	60
R21	135
K- and F-series	69
T32	10
Misc. (F-, R-series)	45

These by no means encompass all of the funding mechanisms of the NIH, but they are the most common and ubiquitous across centers and institutes. Now, let's look at the breakdown for NCCAM (Figure 1).

It should also be noted that the NIH funds its grants by the fiscal year. Consequently, a five-year grant is, in reality, made up of five one-year awards. The difference is that investigators do not have to compete for the renewal of their grants during the years encompassed by them. Rather, they simply have to submit progress reports, and, if reasonable progress is being made, the NIH will usually rubber-stamp the renewal of the grants. These are called "noncompetitive renewals," appropriately enough. The suffixes (-01, -02, -03, etc.) tell us which year of the grant is represented. At the end of the grant period, for R01 and other mechanism, (but not, for example, R21 grants, which are meant to be followed up by other mechanisms), the investigator can either submit a competitive renewal for a continuation of the grant or let the grant lapse.

We see from the above chart that NCCAM funded two new and nine ongoing P01 grants and 14 new and 47 ongoing R01 grants, but a more illuminating analysis comes when we look at the breakdown of general topics being covered in the P01, R01, R21, and training grants. I'm going to take the liberty of concentrating on studies of herbal remedies or dietary

Figure 2. General Topics Covered in R01, P01, and Training Mechanisms

NCCAM grant topic	Number of grants awarded
Herbs, supplements, dietary interventions	109
Modalities considered "CAM" for unclear reasons	12
CAM usage/promotion (not counting fellowships)	13
True "CAM" (chiropractic, craniosacral, prolotherapy, homeopathy, etc.)	61
Centers and fellowship programs	28

supplements or manipulations (mainly because these are the grants that could easily be funded by one of several other NIH institutes), other modalities that are considered "alternative" for unclear reasons (such as studies of various light therapies on different diseases), studies of CAM usage (many of which seem designed to promote CAM usage), true "alternative therapies" (homeopathy, chiropractic, etc.), and then funding for training programs. A caveat is that not everyone will agree with which studies I chose for each group, but the relative numbers are such that minor quibbles on a few studies will not change the overall trend. Finally, I'm going to concentrate mainly on the R01, P01, and training mechanisms (Figure 2).

NCCAM-Funded Studies Wrongly Classify Treatments and Support Preposterous Theories

What we can see from this is that by far the largest category of NCCAM grants for research not related to small businesses is a topic that could just as easily be funded by numerous other institutes or centers within the NIH: The study of herbal remedies, which, when you come right down to it is nothing more than the study of natural products, and studies of dietary manipulations to treat disease and improve health. If you peruse the list, you'll see numerous studies of chromium supplementation, ginkgo biloba, saw palmetto, various dietary manipulations, and similar studies. Since when did the study of natural products and diet become "alternative"? There is no good reason why these sorts of proposals need a special "CAM" center to fund them or why they could not be evaluated by the appropriate study sections in the appropriate disease-specific institute of the NIH.

Then there are a number of other studies (you may disagree with me about the specific studies chosen) that examine physical treatments that are considered "alternative" for unclear reasons, studies such as near infrared therapy or the effects of blue light on alertness. There's no reason why such studies need to be under the rubric of "alternative" or "complementary" medicine, either. These are the same sorts of studies that "conventional" physicians have been doing for decades. Indeed, when it comes to natural products and herbal remedies, I suspect some pharmacologists, dieticians, and medicinal chemists probably look at NCCAM as easy money (or, in this disastrously tight NIH funding environment, at least less torture to get) if they just slap together a project to study the most popular herb *du jour*. Finally, there are the 28 grants funding either fellowships or large collaborative CAM centers or projects and 13 funding studies that either examine CAM usage or seem custom-made to promote CAM usage, such as this study of the effect of increased coverage of CAM therapies by insurance companies.

That just leaves approximately 61 P01-, R01-, or R21-level grants that seem to look at therapies that might truly be called "CAM" (at least by NCCAM's definition). These are, not surprisingly, weighted towards acupuncture or acupressure (17 grants), mind-body interactions (15, with a huge emphasis on "mindfulness," a distinctly religious concept), and then assorted miscellaneous CAM therapies that constitute a grab bag of mostly unrelated modalities. There are also some rather disturbing grants here, a few of which look as though they couldn't get through an Institutional Review Board (IRB) review. For example, there is actually a grant to fund the study of acupuncture for acute spinal cord injury. I wish I were joking. It even pulls the usual acupuncture trick of including electrical stimulation (which, by the way, is not acupuncture, but rather transcutaneous electric nerve stimulation, a decidedly conventional therapy that has been well studied to treat chronic pain) as part of it.

Worst of all, there are two grants to study arguably the most scientifically implausible of all CAM modalities, homeopathy. For instance, there is an R21 grant funding a study called Polysomnography [sleep study] in Homeopathic Remedy Effects. Yes, you have it right. Your tax dollars are going to fund at least a study this year on homeopathic remedies (aka water). But it's even worse than that. There was actually awarded an R21 grant to study homeopathic dilution and succussion and how they affect the dose-response curve of homeopathic remedies. This latter grant actually proposes to study whether succussion (the vigorous shaking done with each homeopathic dilution), which claim homeopaths is necessary to "potentize" their remedies, affects the dose-response characteristics of homeopathic remedies up to 30C dilution (30 times 100-fold, or a dilution factor of 1×10^{-60}). This is a dilution factor many orders of magnitude larger than Avogadro's number, which makes a 30C homeopathic remedy nothing but water. Period. In fact, the investigators are actually going to compare stirring with succussion to see whether succussion, as homeopaths claim, improves the dose-response curve. It beggars the imagination that such a project was actually seriously considered and then scored highly by a study section. There can also be found grants studying seriously dubious modalities such as craniosacral therapy, prolotherapy, and even *qi gong* for treating cocaine addiction. Truly, it's like studying whether eye of newt or pixie dust is more efficacious in curing cancer! . . .

NCCAM Is Biased Toward Promoting CAM

As two of my co-bloggers Wally Sampson and Kimball Atwood IV have pointed out, NCCAM was created not because of any groundswell of support from the scientific community. Rather, it was CAM-friendly legislators who foisted it upon the NIH and made sure that its budget skyrocketed—at least until the recent flattening and decline of the NIH budget put the brakes on. It doesn't seem to matter if a bona fide scientist is placed in charge, either. For example, Dr. Stephen Straus was the director of NCCAM from 1999 to just last year, and he was a hard-core scientist who promised to "explore CAM healing practices in the context of rigorous science, to educate and train CAM researchers and to disseminate authoritative information about CAM to the public." Yet that is not what has happened. Recently, it was announced that Dr. Straus's replacement would be Josephine [P.] Briggs, MD, another accomplished researcher with a strong CV [curriculum vitae] making similar promises. Can she deliver on them?

It's highly unlikely.

Here's why. First, she has only minimal control over who is appointed to the two councils charged with advising the director on matters related to research funding and clinical trials, and, in any case, the council is mandated to be constituted as follows:

> Of the 18 appointed members, 12 shall be selected from among the leading representatives of the health and scientific disciplines (including not less than 2 individuals who are leaders in the fields of public health and the behavioral

NCCAM Conducts Unnecessary Research and Promotes Pseudoscience

Even though NCCAM [the National Center for Complementary and Alternative Medicine] is incredibly friendly to pseudoscience, it has still failed to "validate" a single alternative medicine. The closest it's come is for various natural products, but testing plants and herbs for medicinal compounds is nothing that can't be done in all the other institutes and centers that make up the NIH [National Institutes of Health]. It does not need a special center. . . .

CAM-friendly legislators like Tom Harkin are being used to give CAM supporters a forum in the halls of power to push their agenda. There, they do their best to falsely conflate disease "prevention" with alternative medicine by emphasizing diet and exercise while hiding the bizarre methodologies in CAM, such as *Reiki*, homeopathy, and the like, knowing that if they are successful, after they become the accepted "experts" in diet, exercise, and nutrition that they can bring the woo [ideas considered irrational or based on flimsy evidence] in later in increasing doses.

Be very, very afraid. The age of scientific endarkenment could well be on its way in medicine.

Orac, "Senator Tom Harkin:
NCCAM and Inviting the Four Horseman of the
Woo-pocalypse into the Senate," Respectful Insolence,
March 3, 2009. http://scienceblogs.com.

or social sciences) relevant to the activities of the NCCAM, particularly representatives of the health and scientific disciplines in the area of complementary and alternative medicine. Nine of the members shall be practitioners licensed in one or more of the major systems with which the center is involved.

In other words, they must be CAM practitioners and "leaders" in the field. It's unlikely that such a group will support rigorous science that might threaten their livelihood, and indeed they don't. In fact, its stated mission notwithstanding, NCCAM was never originally intended as a means of rigorously investigating CAM therapies but was rather as a government agency to give these therapies the patina of credibility and respectability that they can't earn through science. Dr. Straus may have tried to do what he said he would do during his tenure, but it clearly just didn't work. He couldn't change NCCAM. Moreover, no matter what he did, he couldn't win either way. On the one hand, he was criticized by scientists and physicians who support science- and evidence-based medicine (like me) for allowing highly dubious studies to be funded, while on the other hand he was castigated for being too scientifically rigorous and not being a CAM practitioner because CAM advocates didn't like his emphasis on determining whether their therapies worked or not. The same thing appears to be true of Dr. Briggs. . . .

CAM advocates . . . don't want truly rigorous scientific studies to determine if these therapies work. They want studies that assume that these therapies work and then simply look at utilization and cost-effectiveness. They want funding of fellowships in CAM (taught, of course, by true believers). In brief, they want CAM promotion.

This is why we can only hope that the NIH really is trying to bury NCCAM. There's nothing that NCCAM does, other than its advocacy for CAM therapies in academic medicine, that couldn't be done as well or much better by other institutes and centers of the NIH appropriate to each question. This is particularly true for the study of herbal remedies and dietary interventions, neither of which are "alternative" except when claims are made that diet or herbs can, for example, cure cancer. Unfortunately, as protected as it is by powerful legislators, the best we can hope for is a career scientist like Dr. Briggs trying to slow NCCAM's descent into pseudoscience. It can't last forever, though. Sooner or later a true believer *will* be appointed director at NCCAM. It's virtually inevitable. The only thing keeping that from happening, I'd guess, is that the most prominent CAM practitioners (like Andrew Weil, for instance) make far too much money to be easily willing to take a huge pay cut to work for NCCAM. When that day comes, any pretense of rigorous science taking into account scientific plausibility will fly out the window.

> *"Critics of alternative medicine . . . argue that the field's more plausible interventions—such as diet, relaxation, yoga and botanical remedies—can be studied just as well in other parts of NIH, where they would need to compete head-to-head with conventional research projects."*

The Value of the National Center for Complementary and Alternative Medicine Is Unclear

David Brown

David Brown is a staff writer for the Washington Post. *In the following viewpoint, Brown reports on the conflict over the funding of the National Center for Complementary and Alternative Medicine (NCCAM). Some scientists have always objected to the existence of NCCAM, Brown explains, and as the US economy has worsened and the budget for the National Institutes of Health*

(NIH) has decreased, the objections have grown more strenuous. Scientists accuse NCCAM of wasting NIH funds on "pseudo-science," and argue that the few NCCAM studies that do have scientific merits could easily be moved into other areas of the NIH. The majority of the objections to NCCAM funding have come in the form of Internet blog posts, but Brown indicates that as Congress continues to debate government funding for health care, the role of NCCAM may become the topic of more wide-spread debate. Brown relates that the majority of studies conducted by NCCAM have yielded negative or inconclusive results, which NCCAM supporters point to as evidence that the center is using scientific, objective measures and is not advocating alternative and complementary treatments, and which NCCAM detractors point to as supporting their view that the agency is wasting taxpayer dollars on unproven treatments.

As you read, consider the following questions:

1. What was NIH director and Nobel laureate Harold Varmus's proposal for funding alternative medicine research in 1998, according to Brown?

2. What disparaging label do opponents of alternative medicine use to describe it, according to the viewpoint?

3. What does the viewpoint state was the effect of Reiki on rats who were stressed by loud noise?

The impending national discussion about broadening access to health care, improving medical practice and saving money is giving a group of scientists an opening to make a once-unthinkable proposal: Shut down the National Center for Complementary and Alternative Medicine [NCCAM] at the National Institutes of Health [NIH].

NCCAM Has a History of Offending Scientists

The notion that the world's best-known medical research agency sponsors studies of homeopathy, acupuncture, therapeutic touch and herbal medicine has always rankled many scientists. That the idea for its creation 17 years ago came from a U.S. senator newly converted to alternative medicine's promise didn't help.

Although NCCAM has a comparatively minuscule budget and although it is a "center" rather than an "institute," making it officially second-class in the NIH pantheon, the principle is what mattered. But as NIH's budget has flattened in recent years, better use for NCCAM's money has also become an issue.

"With a new administration and President [Barack] Obama's stated goal of moving science to the forefront, now is the time for scientists to start speaking up about issues that concern us," Steven Salzberg, a genome researcher and computational biologist at the University of Maryland, said last week [in March 2009]. "One of our concerns is that NIH is funding pseudoscience."

Salzberg suggested that NCCAM be defunded on an electronic bulletin board that the Obama transition team set up to solicit ideas after November's election. The proposal generated 218 comments, most of them in favor, before the bulletin board closed on Jan. 19.

NCCAM has grown steadily since its founding in 1992, largely at the insistence of Sen. Tom Harkin (D-Iowa), as the Office of Alternative Medicine (OAM) with a budget of $2 million. In 1998, NIH director and Nobel laureate Harold Varmus pushed to have all alternative medicine research done through NIH's roughly two dozen institutes, with OAM coordinating, and in some cases paying for, the studies. Harkin parried with legislation that turned OAM into a higher-status "center" (although not a full-fledged "institute"), and boosted its budget from $20 million to $50 million. NCCAM's budget this year is about $122 million.

Research in alternative medicine is done elsewhere at NIH, notably in the National Cancer Institute, whose Office of Cancer Complementary and Alternative Medicine also has a budget of $122 million.

The entire NIH alternative medicine portfolio is about $300 million a year, out of a total budget of about $29 billion. (NIH will get an additional $10.4 billion in economic stimulus money over the next two years, of which $31 million is expected to go to NCCAM.)

Critics of alternative medicine say the vast majority of studies of homeopathy, acupuncture, therapeutic touch and other treatments based on unconventional understandings of physiology and disease have shown little or no effect. Further, they argue that the field's more plausible interventions—such as diet, relaxation, yoga and botanical remedies—can be studied just as well in other parts of NIH, where they would need to compete head-to-head with conventional research projects.

The critics say that alternative medicine (also known as "complementary" and "integrative" medicine, and disparagingly labeled "woo" by opponents) doesn't need or deserve its own home at NIH.

"What has happened is that the very fact that NIH is supporting a study is used to market alternative medicine," said Steven Novella, a neurologist at Yale School of Medicine and editor of the website Science-Based Medicine, where much of the anti-NCCAM discussion is taking place. "It is used to lend an appearance of legitimacy to treatments that are not legitimate."

Beyond the Blogosphere

So far, most of the debate has occurred in the blogosphere. But as health care reform moves toward center stage, so may this fight.

At a Senate committee hearing on integrative medicine held Feb. 26, Harkin said: "I want to lay down a . . . marker: If we fail to seize this unique opportunity to adopt a pragmatic, integrative approach to health care, then that, too, would constitute a serious failure."

At the hearing, Harkin introduced Berkley W. Bedell, a six-term Democratic congressman from Iowa who retired in 1987 after contracting Lyme disease. Bedell credits alternative therapies for his recovery from that infection and later from prostate cancer. He helped convince the Iowa senator of alternative medicine's promise.

Nevertheless, Harkin said he was somewhat disappointed in NCCAM's work.

"One of the purposes when we drafted that legislation in 1992 . . . was to investigate and validate alternative approaches. Quite frankly, I must say it's fallen short," he told the committee.

"I think quite frankly that in this center, and previously in the office before it, most of its focus has been on disproving things, rather than seeking out and proving things."

Critics say this shows Harkin's lack of understanding of scientific inquiry, which tests hypotheses (with negative results as informative as positive ones) but doesn't intentionally attempt to "validate approaches." NCCAM's current director, Josephine P. Briggs, agrees that hypothesis-testing is the proper function of the center.

"We are not advocates for these modalities," she said last week. "We are trying to bring rigor to their study and make sure the science is objective."

Even so, Harkin was on to something: Most of NCCAM's results have been negative or inconclusive, not positive and encouraging.

For example, a randomized controlled trial of the botanical echinacea published in 2003 found it was ineffective in treating upper respiratory infections (although it did cause more rashes). In a study from last year, neither the Japanese "palm healing" therapy known as Reiki, nor sham Reiki, reduced the symptoms of fibromyalgia, a chronic pain syndrome. A study in December comparing real and sham acupuncture in 162 cancer patients who'd undergone surgery found no difference in their levels of pain.

At the same time, it's difficult to determine the clinical implications of some of the positive studies.

For example, Reiki—but not sham treatment—blunted the rise in heart rate, but not the rise in blood pressure, in rats put under stress by loud noise. Therapeutic touch, a different modality, increased the growth of normal bone cells in culture dishes, but decreased the growth of bone cancer cells.

Studies Funded by NCCAM Often Focus on Practical Medical Applications

Many NCCAM-funded studies examine not the effectiveness of alternative medicine but its use, and how it affects the interaction of practitioners and patients. The idea that the center is spending lots of money running large clinical trials of such practices as homeopathy and ayurvedic medicine "is a misperception," the director said. She noted that most such proposals lack methodological rigor and aren't approved.

A physician and kidney specialist who never used alternative medicine in her practice, Briggs said "mind-body management for pain control and stress reduction" is a large topic of the research at the moment, with mindfulness, meditation, yoga and tai chi all under study.

"Some of the way these approaches work is through 'positive expectancy,' which is part of a placebo effect," she said.

Indeed, many of NCCAM's critics view complementary medicine as nothing more than the placebo effect dressed up in a dozen different costumes.

Carlo Calabrese, a researcher at the National College of Natural Medicine in Portland, Ore., one of the country's five naturopathic medical schools, isn't one of them. But even if one were to concede that view, he thinks the field is still worth studying.

Although the overall effect of therapies such as homeopathy and acupuncture may be small, individual response can be large. The route to the placebo effect—if that's what it mostly is—also varies in method and efficiency.

"What can be done to generate a better placebo? Why isn't that an interesting and valid area of investigation?" said Calabrese, who was on NCCAM's advisory council from 2004 to 2007. "Here we have a totally harmless intervention that seems to get a better result in some people than others. Why wouldn't you want to study that?"

> *"The Dietary Supplement Labeling Act would improve the information available to consumers and curb the prevalence of drinks and foods that are masquerading as dietary supplements as a means of avoiding reviews and regulation by the FDA."*

Expanding Labeling Requirements Would Better Inform Consumers About Safe Supplement Use

The Office of Senator Dick Durbin

Dick Durbin is a Democratic senator representing the state of Illinois, and Richard Blumenthal is a Democratic senator representing the state of Connecticut. In the following viewpoint, background information is provided on Durbin and Blumenthal's proposed Dietary Supplement Labeling Act, which they introduced on June 30, 2011. Durbin and Blumenthal argue that certain foods and beverages containing potentially unsafe levels of botanical ingredients are marketed as dietary supplements to take advantage of the relatively lax laws governing the regulation of these products by the US Food and Drug Administration (FDA). The proposed legislation would protect consumers, the senators argue, by giving the FDA the authority to determine which products should be regulated as foods and beverages, and also by requiring that dietary supplements be registered with the FDA. Further, Durbin and Blumenthal add, the Dietary Supplement Labeling Act would require that supplement manufacturers clearly state any potential risks associated with the ingredients in their product on the label and display a warning label if a product contains any ingredient that has the potential to cause serious adverse reactions. This would, the senators assert, enable the FDA to identify any potential safety concerns and provide consumers with more accurate information about the products they choose to purchase and use.

As you read, consider the following questions:

1. What potentially dangerous dietary supplement do Lazy Cakes, Kush Cakes, and Lulla Pies contain that Durbin argues should be regulated as a food additive?

2. In what year did the FDA issue a ten-year plan for implementing the Dietary Supplement Health and Education Act of 1994, according to the viewpoint?

3. What new information, other than warnings of adverse events, would supplement manufacturers be legally required to list on their product labels under the Dietary Supplement Labeling Act, according to the viewpoint?

U.S. senators Dick Durbin (D-IL) and Richard Blumenthal (D-CT) today [June 30, 2011] introduced legislation that would ensure that consumers have the information they need to distinguish between products that are safe and others that contain potentially dangerous ingredients which haven't been approved by the Food and Drug Administration (FDA). The Dietary Supplement Labeling Act would improve the information available to consumers and curb the prevalence of drinks

and foods that are masquerading as dietary supplements as a means of avoiding reviews and regulation by the FDA.

"Walk down the aisle of your local convenience store and you will see products targeting young people with names like Lazy Cakes, Drank and Monster Energy Drink," said Durbin. "These products market themselves as dietary supplements that are safe ways to relax or get a boost of energy, when in reality they are foods and beverages taking advantage of the more relaxed safety standards for dietary supplements. My bill would help curb this unsafe practice."

"Consumers deserve to know what adverse effects these products can have on their health and well-being," said Blumenthal. "Truth in labeling and honest marketing is critical to consumer safety—especially in products targeted towards young people—and should be required as an industry standard."

Foods Containing Dietary Supplements Should Be Clearly Labeled and Regulated

Today's legislation would require the FDA to establish a clear definition of which products are foods and should be regulated as such and which products are meant to be health aids and should be regulated as dietary supplements.

Last month, Durbin raised concerns with the Food and Drug Administration about baked goods—such as Lazy Cakes, Kush Cakes, and Lulla Pies—containing melatonin that, because they are marketed as dietary supplements, do not require approval by the FDA for use as additives in food. Under current law, it is the choice of the manufacturer as to whether a product is classified as a food or as a dietary supplement. In January 2010, the FDA issued a warning letter to the manufacturer of Drank for selling a beverage containing melatonin. The manufacturer responded by changing the labeling of Drank from a "beverage" to a "dietary supplement," which do not require approval by the FDA for use as additives in food.

This is not the first time the FDA has been asked to clarify its authority to regulate certain dietary supplements and food additives. In January 2000, the FDA issued a 10-year plan to implement the Dietary Supplement Health and Education Act of 1994 (DSHEA), which identified the need to clarify the distinction between conventional foods and dietary supplements. Moreover, U.S. [Government] Accountability Office (GAO) reports in July 11, 2000, and January 29, 2009, recommended the FDA clarify the boundary.

Labeling and Regulating Supplements Would Better Inform Consumers About Risks and Benefits

"It's important to note most products labeled as dietary supplements are legitimate health aids. I take a daily vitamin just as millions of Americans do," said Durbin. "My gripe is not with the array of vitamins available at health stores across the nation; my gripe is with products labeled as 'dietary supplements' whose ingredients have not been deemed safe by the FDA but are found on store shelves right next to conventional food and beverages. The current system favors the manufacturers of these products to the detriment of consumers—and that needs to change."

Today's legislation would also improve the information available to consumers by requiring dietary supplement manufacturers to register dietary supplement products to the FDA and provide a description of each dietary supplement, a list of ingredients, and a copy of the label. This would allow the FDA to track how many dietary supplements are on the market and how many products contain certain ingredients, increasing their capacity to inform manufacturers of possible safety concerns. It would also require product labels to include warnings associated with adverse events of specific ingredients, weight of those ingredients per serving, and a batch number for easier recall.

In 2006, Durbin led a bipartisan effort to enact legislation requiring manufacturers to report serious adverse events related to consuming dietary supplements, enhancing the FDA's ability to identify and respond more quickly to potential health problems. The Dietary Supplement Labeling Act would build on that by requiring dietary supplement manufacturers to disclose the known risks of ingredients and display a mandatory warning if the product contains a dietary ingredient that may cause potentially serious adverse events. Labels would also have to include the batch number, which would help the FDA identify and recall contaminated products.

> "Dick Durbin, in his heart of hearts, would like to . . . try to roll back dietary supplements law to something he wishes it was, which is a limited choice of dietary supplements to consumers."

Expanding Labeling Requirements for Dietary Supplements Would Punish Consumers and Manufacturers

Hank Schultz and Todd Runestad

Hank Schultz is the managing editor of Functional Ingredients *magazine, and Todd Runestad is editor in chief and science editor of the magazine. In the following viewpoint, Schultz and Runestad report that according to experts from the dietary supplement manufacturing industry, the Dietary Supplement Labeling Act proposed by Senator Dick Durbin would place unnecessary and regulatory burdens on manufacturers and would threaten the industry's future viability. The authors report that while manufacturers agree that foods should not be marketed as dietary supplements, they feel that the proposed legislation goes too far by lumping all dietary supplements and manufacturers into the same category. Instead, manufacturers argue, existing laws and regulations should be enforced to prevent problem products from posing a danger to public health. Some natural products industry leaders, the authors reveal, question the motivation behind Durbin's proposed legislation, speculating that the senator may be seeking to circumvent new dietary ingredients guidelines released by the US Food and Drug Administration (FDA) under the Food Safety Modernization Act. Whether or not the bill passes, industry advocates maintain, the negative attention it brings to the industry will likely create unfounded concern about dietary supplement safety among consumers, despite the fact that the industry has a sterling safety record and that adverse events caused directly by dietary supplements are rare.*

As you read, consider the following questions:

1. What dollar figure does the viewpoint cite for total US consumer sales of energy drinks in 2010?

2. What specific brand of energy shot does Durbin mention in his announcement of his proposed legislation, according to the viewpoint?

3. How many deaths per year does the FDA report are caused by food-borne pathogens, according to the viewpoint?

Citing problems with the marketing and labeling of energy drinks and melatonin brownies, Sen. Dick Durbin (D-Ill.) announced on Tuesday, June 27, [2011,] that he intends to introduce the Dietary Supplement Labeling Act this week mandating sweeping new regulations for the dietary supplements and functional foods industries.

"You can't make it to the cash register without encountering flashy advertising displays for energy supplements like Rockstar Energy Drink and 5-hour Energy," Durbin said in a press release announcing the bill. "These products, which market themselves as dietary supplements that offer a boost of energy, are foods and beverages taking advantage of the less stringent safety standards for dietary supplements under current law."

Among other things, Durbin's bill would mandate the U.S. Food and Drug Administration (FDA) to:

- establish a definition for "conventional foods"

- require increased warning language on labels

- require manufacturers to register dietary supplements with the agency

According to executives from the supplement trade associations, the bill also includes other enhanced registration and labeling requirements the industry would consider either duplicative or excessive—especially given the relatively stellar safety record of supplements.

The Fate of the Entire Supplement Industry Is at Stake

One fairly unprecedented aspect of the bill would require disclosure of the exact ingredient amounts of proprietary formulations. Would such a move strike at the heart of a company's intellectual property portfolio?

Absolutely, said Michael McGuffin, president of the American Herbal Products Association (AHPA). "It doesn't surprise me," McGuffin added. "Dick Durbin, in his heart of hearts, would like to reduce back to tablets the dietary supplements class and try to roll back dietary supplements law to something he wishes it was, which is a limited choice of dietary supplements to consumers."

Right in the crosshairs of the bill is the energy drink and energy shot market. According to *Nutrition Business Journal* estimates, U.S. consumer sales of energy drinks totaled $6.3 billion in 2010, while sales of the newer energy shot products hit $1.3 billion last year.

"Durbin lays out that energy drinks are little time bombs waiting to go off in the hands of consumers who don't understand what these products are, their dangers, their risks, and this is a travesty that requires federal regulation to fix," said Loren Israelsen, executive director of the United Natural Products Alliance (UNPA). "It's a fairly sexy headline."

Durbin identified the Drank beverage, which contains melatonin, as a product that, in his view, used loopholes in the regulatory structure to avoid FDA sanction. In response to a January 2010 FDA warning letter stating that melatonin was an unapproved food additive, the manufacturer of Drank relabeled the product as a dietary supplement.

Enforce Existing Regulations Instead of Adding New Regulations

"We don't want people producing things that are masquerading as supplements," said John Gay, executive director and CEO of the Natural Products Association (NPA). "We agree with him on that. But we certainly draw the line on saying that the entire supplements industry needs new regulations laid on top of it to address a small segment of the universe that should be addressed in large part through existing law."

"If this bill is the solution [to the problem of labeling of energy and relaxation beverages] it goes way beyond the problem it is focusing on," Gay added.

In announcing his intention to unveil this bill, Durbin also specifically called out 5-hour Energy, the leading brand in the energy shot category. Current law states that such products are not to be represented as foods or beverages. To that end, these products contain a supplements facts box and not a nutrition facts box on the back of labels. (Representatives from 5-hour Energy could not be reached for comment.)

According to McGuffin, products like energy shots conform to the letter of the law. "Congress intended us to sell supplement products in delivery systems other than pills or tinctures," said McGuffin. "They tolerate things like energy bars that are sold as dietary supplements."

Although the energy shot category is likely fine, what of energy drinks?

"That's a good question," said McGuffin. "Caffeine is GRAS [generally recognized as safe] for foods, vitamins and amino acids are food. If you're a functional food company marketing a food with a nutrition facts panel, you have to comply with food regulations. We have a broader list of ingredients we can sell in supplements. A company that tries to deliver dietary supplements in a food form must not represent the product as a food in order to comply with the law as it is today."

The Timing and Motivation of Durbin's Proposed Legislation Are Suspicious

So why is Durbin releasing this bill now? According to UNPA's Israelsen, the senator's timing is concerning. FDA is mandated by the Food Safety Modernization Act (FSMA) to release its long-awaited new dietary ingredients (NDI) guidance document by July 3 or the next business day (180 days after the passage of FSMA). That document is expected to address many of the concerns raised by Durbin in terms of what ingredients should be subject to NDI filings, a process that focuses on safety.

"Here we are, all dressed up, ready to go to the party, waiting to see what FDA comes up with," Israelsen said. "But— and this is my view—Durbin is saying he's going to head the NDI guidance off at the pass and make the discussion about how the industry can't be trusted."

The keen focus in Congress on the state of federal finances, while presumably not affecting the July deadline for

The Dietary Supplement Labeling Act of 2011 Threatens Consumers' Freedom and Companies' Viability

Under the cover of the July 4th [2011] holiday, Senator Richard Durbin (D-Illinois) and the FDA [US Food and Drug Administration] launched an unprecedented and coordinated assault on the dietary supplement industry—in essence a direct attack on consumers who rely on dietary supplements to support their health.

Without a massive consumer protest of this abhorrent abuse of regulatory power, consumers will be denied access to many dietary supplements they currently take. Furthermore, the cost of dietary supplements will skyrocket due to the unnecessary regulatory burden imposed upon dietary supplement companies, the legal wars that will go on for years, and the reduction in competition that currently keeps prices low.

While there are many political forces in play, it is clear that one of the main goals of this attack is to allow the pharmaceutical companies to take over the dietary supplement industry.

*Byron J. Richards, "Senator Durbin and the FDA
Viciously Attack Dietary Supplements," NewsWithViews.com,
July 26, 2011. www.newswithviews.com.*

NDIs, could still wreak havoc on the responsible part of the industry. That's because congressional Republicans are looking to strip funding for the FSMA.

"We still have an affirmative obligation to abide by the law," said McGuffin. "If Congress takes money away for inspections, it doesn't mean I don't have to comply with the law.

It means companies doing everything to comply will have no competitive advantage over less-conforming competitors because there are no inspectors."

"Will it pass or not? I don't know," said Israelsen. "Is it a dangerous bill? Yes."

"The ideas are cruise missile shots at DSHEA, from a member of Congress who has the horsepower and the motive to advance the bill," he added.

Other observers see the current political climate in Washington, D.C., as being antithetical to the bill's chances. "Any bill with anything other than finances doesn't have a lot of interest in the 112th Congress," said McGuffin. "If Senator Durbin does not have a good range of cosponsors, especially with our industry champions like Sen. [Orrin] Hatch, the likelihood of this passing is low."

The Stellar Safety Record of Dietary Supplements Contradicts Critics' Warnings

Of course, even if the bill does not pass, Durbin will be able to use its creation and promotion to stir up headlines raising questions about the safety of dietary supplements, while also trumpeting his own position as a crusader for consumer safety.

Despite assertions from Durbin and others, the vast majority of dietary supplements—and the ingredients that go into them—are safe. All one has to do is look at data from the FDA's Adverse Events Reporting System [AERS] to see that.

According to AERS data, the FDA received 33 reports of deaths associated with dietary supplements in 2008 and 2009. Of course, as McGuffin notes, association does not connote causation.

"One of the cases was an 80-year-old with cod liver oil in his medicine cabinet when he died, that got reported as an associated event," said McGuffin. "On the whole, the class of dietary supplement products is very safe. The FDA says there are 3,000 deaths a year caused by food-borne pathogens. There are more than 400,000 deaths associated with pharmaceutical drugs."

Periodical and Internet Sources Bibliography

The following articles have been selected to supplement the diverse views presented in this chapter.

Mike Adams	"2009 in Review: A Year of FDA Censorship, Big Pharma Crimes and Celebrity Drug Deaths," NaturalNews.com, January 1, 2010. www.naturalnews.com.
Joseph K. Dier	"S.O.S. from the FDA: A Cry for Help in the World of Unregulated Dietary Supplements," *Albany Law Review*, vol. 74, no. 1, September 22, 2010.
Chris Gonsalves	"Now Gov't Trying to Ban Sale of Your Supplements," Newsmax.com, July 29, 2011. www.newsmax.com.
David Gorski	"Why Senator Tom Harkin Should Be Considered a Public Health Menace," *NCCAM Watch*, May 3, 2011. www.nccamwatch.org.
Michael Johnsen	"Dietary Supplement Labeling Act Draws Opposition from CRN," Drug Store News, July 5, 2011. www.drugstorenews.com.
Michelle Minton	"The Coming War on Vitamins," *Washington Times*, July 28, 2011.
Jennifer Nelson and Katherine Zeratsky	"Dietary Supplements: Greater Accountability Needed," *Nutrition-wise Blog*, January 18, 2011. www.mayoclinic.com.
Steven Novella	"Our Visit with NCCAM," Science-Based Medicine, April 7, 2010. www.sciencebasedmedicine.org.
Bill Sardi	"News Media, in League with Government, Begins Orchestrated Smear Campaign against Dietary Supplements," LewRockwell.com, September 3, 2011. http://lewrockwell.com.

For Further Discussion

Chapter 1

1. Dana Ullman argues that conventional medicine is fundamentally flawed because it is focused upon treating symptoms and attacking disease rather than working like homeopathy does, supporting the body's own natural defenses to cure disease. He also maintains that pharmaceutical companies selectively interpret research data that supports their desired outcomes. What evidence does he offer to support this contention? Does the manner in which he presents his argument strengthen or weaken this claim that homeopathy is effective and is validated by sound scientific research, and why? How does Ullman's approach to disproving the claims of critics of homeopathy differ from Edzard Ernst's approach to disproving the claims of homeopathy proponents? Which is more successful, and why?

2. Ted Burnham maintains that because the subjects in research trials who receive sham acupuncture respond just as favorably to treatment as those who receive real acupuncture, any positive outcomes from acupuncture are due only to the placebo effect and all acupuncture is ineffective. He attributes the subjects' positive responses to the extra attention and care they receive from the person performing the acupuncture. John Amaro, however, concludes that the sham versus real acupuncture trials are flawed and unreliable because researchers are not using proper acupuncture technique and lack a fundamental understanding of acupuncture. Which author's interpretation of the study data seems the most plausible to you, and why? Does Burnham provide enough data to support his argu-

ment? Why or why not? Is Amaro's contention that it may be impossible to conduct blind or double-blind studies of acupuncture supported by the evidence he provides? If so, how, and if not, why not?

3. Both Elmer M. Cranton and Saul Green accuse the other of falsely representing and manipulating research study data regarding the efficacy of chelation therapy. Which author does a better job of presenting data to support his own views, and why? Which author is most effective at disproving the other's claims, and why?

Chapter 2

1. Rahul Parikh points to cultural and psychological characteristics that motivate people to pursue alternative medical treatments. Does the fact that he provides a historical context for his argument make it more or less persuasive? Why or why not? Is Parikh's overall message either supportive or dismissive of alternative medicine? Offer evidence to illustrate your conclusion.

2. Liz Szabo reports that there is widespread and often detrimental belief in celebrity health advice because, as medical experts assert, people often feel more personally connected to celebrities than to scientists or physicians. Is this true for you? Would you be likely to follow a celebrity's health advice without further investigation? Why or why not? If you did choose to investigate a celebrity's claims, what source would you use to verify the information, and why?

Chapter 3

1. David Katz dismisses the argument that using complementary and alternative medical treatments that have not been proven effective via randomized controlled trials runs contrary to the scientific method, and he contends that it is really those who claim that they have proof that untested alternative treatments do not work who are not

following the scientific method. What do you think of Katz's argument that not having evidence that something is true does not mean that it is false? Apply this reasoning to a situation in your own life. Does it seem valid? Why or why not?

2. Ben Kavoussi maintains that acupuncture is neither effective nor derived from an ancient medical tradition, and that doctors and university medical centers who research and promote the use of alternative medical treatments such as acupuncture are guilty of abandoning their commitments to their patients' best interests in pursuit of wealth. Does Kavoussi's argument regarding the origins of modern acupuncture support his contention about the motivations of doctors and medical centers that promote its use? Does he demonstrate compelling evidence that acupuncture proponents are motivated by greed? Explain.

3. Steve Silberman's viewpoint proposes that treatment with placebos is ethical—and has been proven to still be successful—if patients are informed that they are receiving placebos at the outset, and he contends that doctors should utilize these treatments more frequently, especially in cases where other treatments are not available or have undesirable or risky side effects. Eliezer Sobel maintains that the use of placebos is not without the potential for negative side effects, since withdrawal symptoms can result when the effect wears off and that the belief that something is harmful can have the opposite, or "nocebo" effect and produce negative outcomes. Do you think the use of placebos for treatment is practical and/or ethical? Why or why not? Would you be willing to try a placebo treatment, and do you think it would be helpful for you? Why or why not? Consider how you might feel if you discovered that you had been treated with a placebo when you thought you had been taking a prescribed medication.

What effect might such an experience have on your trust in your doctor, medical science, and your own perceptions?

Chapter 4

1. David Gorski finds fault with what he sees as a bias toward promoting alternative medicine within the National Center for Complementary and Alternative Medicine (NCCAM), arguing that this degrades scientific credibility and as such represents an unethical and unproductive use of taxpayer dollars. David Brown's viewpoint presents the view of one researcher, Carlo Calabrese, who maintains that even if all of NCCAM's research shows that all alternative treatments are nothing more than placebos that this is still valuable information that can have positive implications for practical medical use. Which of these arguments do you find more compelling, and why? What information not provided in either of the viewpoints do you think would help you decide whether the work done at NCCAM is worthwhile? How might that change your opinion of either of the authors' arguments?

2. Dick Durbin and Richard Blumenthal argue that further regulation and oversight of dietary supplements is needed to ensure product safety and protect consumers from potential health dangers. Hank Schultz and Todd Runestad contend that better enforcement of current laws and regulations would be adequate to protect consumers. They also maintain that efforts to enact further restrictions on dietary supplements threaten consumers' choices about their own health and that efforts to hamper dietary supplement sales are motivated by a vested interest in the pharmaceutical and health care industries that are threatened by the competition. Given the evidence provided, how likely are you to use dietary supplements? Do you think your decision is more affected by a fear of contaminated supple-

ments or by a distrust of government or the pharmaceutical industry? What do you think would be the best way to address safety concerns without compromising consumer freedom or business interests? Explain.

Organizations to Contact

The editors have compiled the following list of organizations concerned with the issues debated in this book. The descriptions are derived from materials provided by the organizations. All have publications or information available for interested readers. The list was compiled on the date of publication of the present volume; the information provided here may change. Be aware that many organizations take several weeks or longer to respond to inquiries, so allow as much time as possible.

Alliance for Natural Health (ANH-USA)
1350 Connecticut Avenue NW, Washington, DC   20036
(800) 230-2762 • fax: (202) 315-5837
e-mail: media@anh-usa.org
website: www.anh-usa.org

The Alliance for Natural Health (ANH-USA) is part of an international group that advocates an integrative approach to medicine, a sustainable approach to health and eating, and freedom of choice for consumers of health care and natural products. The ANH-USA acts as a government watchdog to support consumers' rights to pursue a financially and environmentally sustainable lifestyle and choose a preventive health care model; lobbies the US Congress and state legislatures; offers education on issues for the public and the press; and files official comments on proposed court rulings.

American Academy of Medical Acupuncture (AAMA)
1970 E. Grand Avenue, Suite 330
El Segundo, California   90245
(310) 364-0193
e-mail: administrator@medicalacupuncture.org
website: www.medicalacupuncture.org

Members of the American Academy of Medical Acupuncture (AAMA) are licensed physicians who are also trained acupuncturists. Medical acupuncture is the term used to describe acupuncture performed by a licensed physician. The AAMA promotes the utilization of traditional and modern forms of acupuncture along with Western medicine to provide an integrated and comprehensive approach to health care.

American Association of Integrative Medicine (AAIM)

2750 E. Sunshine, Springfield, MO   65804
(877) 718-3053 • fax: (417) 823-9959
website: www.aaimedicine.com

The American Association of Integrative Medicine (AAIM) promotes and advocates for improved clinical outcomes through integrative medicine, linking consumers with providers, and implementing and maintaining training programs and studies to support practitioners in integrative health care. The organization allows integrative practitioners from a variety of backgrounds and disciplines, including medical and osteopathic doctors, to join together to learn and support one another in the development of their practice. The organization supports the preservation of indigenous medicine and publishes a peer-reviewed journal, *The Annals of Psychotherapy & Integrative Health*.

American Chiropractic Association (ACA)

1701 Clarendon Boulevard, Arlington, VA   22209
(703) 276-8800 • fax: (703) 243-2593
e-mail: memberinfo@acatoday.org
website: www.acatoday.org

The American Chiropractic Association (ACA), a professional organization for chiropractors, works to advance understanding and standards of chiropractic methods through lobbying efforts, public relations, increased research, and provision of educational materials. Publications such as ACA News, *Journal of the American Chiropractic Association (JACA) Online, Journal of Manipulative and Physiological Therapeutics (JMPT)*, and *Healthy Living Fact Sheets: Patient Education Pages* provide both professionals and patients with the opportunity to learn more about the benefits of the chiropractic modality.

American College for Advancement in Medicine (ACAM)

8001 Irvine Center Drive, Suite 825, Irvine, CA   92618
(949) 309-3520 • fax: (949) 309-3538
website: www.acamnet.org

The American College for Advancement in Medicine (ACAM) is a not-for-profit corporation dedicated to the education of physicians and other care providers in the use of integrative medicine as part of the organization's larger goal of promoting a health care model that emphasizes preventive medicine and total wellness. ACAM supports integrative medicine research and provides guidance on standards of care as well as on new findings and procedures. The website provides educational and enrichment resources for providers and a searchable directory of integrative health care providers for consumers.

American Council on Science and Health (ACSH)

1995 Broadway, Suite 202, New York, NY   10023-5882
(212) 362-7044 • fax: (212) 362-4919
e-mail: acsh@acsh.org
website: www.acsh.org

The American Council on Science and Health (ACSH) provides consumers with what it views as carefully balanced and accurate information on health- and science-related issues. Through activities such as seminars, press conferences, and coordination with the media, ACSH is dedicated to dispensing unbiased information regarding topics such as alternative medicine, nutrition, pharmaceuticals, and tobacco. The "Facts and Fears" section of the organization's website provides a searchable database of articles published by the organization; other topical ACSH publications can also be browsed and searched.

American Holistic Medical Association (AHMA)

23366 Commerce Park, Suite 101B, Beachwood, OH   44122
(216) 292-6644 • fax: (212) 292-6688

e-mail: info@holisticmedicine.org
website: www.holisticmedicine.org

The American Holistic Medical Association (AHMA) is a professional organization of medical doctors, doctors of osteopathic medicine, medical students who practice or are studying to practice holistic medicine, and licensed practitioners of various alternative medicine modalities, including acupuncture, biofeedback, chelation therapy, energy medicine, and functional medicine. AHMA works to aid these individuals in their careers and to provide information for professionals and the public about holistic practices. Physician and practitioner referrals through the organization's database as well as a guide to choosing a holistic professional are available on the organization's website.

American Medical Association (AMA)
515 N. State Street, Chicago, IL   60610
(800) 621-8335
website: www.ama-assn.org

The American Medical Association (AMA) is a professional organization of physicians that seeks to improve the health of all Americans. The organization provides policy guidelines on pertinent issues in health care and provides an opportunity for doctors to collaborate nationwide in addressing the needs of patients. Issues such as the integration of alternative medicine and the use and regulation of dietary supplements have been addressed in the pages of the AMA's publication, the *Journal of the American Medical Association (JAMA)*.

The Bravewell Collaborative
1818 Oliver Avenue S, Minneapolis, MN   55405
(612) 377-8400
e-mail: info@bravewell.org
website: www.bravewell.org

The Bravewell Collaborative is a philanthropic organization with the mission of increasing the use of integrative medicine in health care. With scholarship programs that encourage young medical students to enter the field of integrative medicine, public education outreach activities, and leadership awards, the Bravewell Collaborative has been at the forefront of promoting improved health care through the cooperation of traditional and alternative medicines. Detailed information about integrative medicine and its relationship to health care is available on the organization's website.

Citizens for Health

1400 Sixteenth Street NW, Suite 101, Washington, DC   20036
e-mail: info@citizens.org
website: www.citizens.org

As a national consumer advocacy organization, Citizens for Health works to ensure that consumers have the opportunity and freedom to choose the type of health care they desire. Through grassroots organization and cooperation with private industry, Citizens for Health promotes the idea that government legislation should always protect the right of individuals to choose their own health services. Current and archived blog posts and current action alerts are available on the organization's website, as is additional information about how individuals can participate in various actions.

Committee for Skeptical Inquiry (CSI)

PO Box 703, Amherst, NY   14226
(716) 636-1425
e-mail: info@csicop.org
website: www.csicop.org

The Committee for Skeptical Inquiry (CSI) is an organization dedicated to evaluating controversial and extraordinary claims using science-based methodology and critical inquiry. Through conferences and publications, CSI encourages skepticism about claims related to such topics as complementary and alternative medicine, astrology and astronomy, and UFOs, until such statements can be proven through objective study. The organization publishes the journal the *Skeptical Inquirer*, and previously published articles can be found on the CSI website.

Federal Trade Commission (FTC)

600 Pennsylvania Avenue NW, Washington, DC   20580
(202) 326-2222
website: www.ftc.gov

The Federal Trade Commission (FTC) is an independent agency within the federal government that seeks to ensure that consumers in the United States receive accurate information about products and services sold to them. Projects and resources are commissioned by the FTC to increase consumer understanding and awareness on health-related claims. Articles and reports concerning complementary and alternative modalities and therapies, as well as dietary supplements, can be found on the FTC website.

Food and Drug Administration (FDA)

560 Fishers Lane, Rockville, MD   20857
(888) 463-6332
website: www.fda.gov

The US Food and Drug Administration (FDA) is the consumer protection agency of the US Department of Health and Human Services that regulates the food and drug products sold to the American public. Vitamins and dietary supplements are among the products the FDA tests using science-based methods to determine their safety and efficacy. FDA ensures that labels provide information about all ingredients included in the product as well as the product's apparent risks and benefits. More detailed information about the projects of the FDA can be found on the agency's website.

National Center for Complementary and Alternative Medicine (NCCAM)

National Institutes of Health, 9000 Rockville Pike
Bethesda, MD   20892
(888) 644-6226 • fax: (866) 464-3616
e-mail: info@nccam.nih.gov
website: http://nccam.nih.gov

The National Center for Complementary and Alternative Medicine (NCCAM) is the branch of the National Institutes of Health (NIH) responsible for addressing issues related to complementary and alternative medicine (CAM) at the federal level. The organization focuses on researching alternative health practices, informing professionals and the public about findings, and encouraging the integration into conventional medicine of CAM modalities that have stood up to rigorous testing and have been deemed acceptable for use. NCCAM's website provides access to numerous fact sheets on CAM practices, as well as video lectures and information about how to order publications.

National Council Against Health Fraud (NCAHF)

(919) 533-6009
e-mail: sbinfo@quackwatch.com
website: www.ncahf.org

National Council Against Health Fraud (NCAHF) is a private nonprofit health agency dedicated to informing the public about health fraud, quackery, and health misinformation, guided by scientific principles and consumer law. The agency advocates regulation and oversight of health-related products and services and rigorous oversight of health care providers and product manufacturers. The website is owned and maintained by board member Stephen Barrett, MD, and provides links to new and archived editions of *NCAHF News, Consumer Health Digest*, and other resources published by the NCAHF and its members. The website also provides links to NCAHF position papers, task force reports, policy statements, and consumer information statements, as well as links to other resources and websites.

Quackwatch

Chatham Crossing, Suite 107/208, 11312 US 15-501 N
Chapel Hill, NC   27517
e-mail: sbinfo@quackwatch.com
website: www.quackwatch.org

Quackwatch is an Internet network of individuals who are concerned with the mission of exposing fraudulent practices and philosophies associated with alternative and complementary medicine. Quackwatch strives to ensure that all claims and advertising relating to health care products and services are appropriately addressed and analyzed. Quackwatch is also dedicated to analyzing information dispensed on the Internet to advance the quality of information most often sought by consumers. Links to topic-specific websites within the network, as well as numerous articles concerning these topics, are available on the Quackwatch website.

World Health Organization (WHO)

Pan American Health Organization (PAHO)
525 Twenty-Third Street NW, Washington, DC   20037
(202) 974-3000 • fax: (202) 974-3663
e-mail: postmaster@paho.org
website: www.paho.org

The World Health Organization (WHO) and its regional office, the Pan American Health Organization (PAHO), are international health organizations within the United Nations charged with ensuring that individuals worldwide are afforded appropriate health care. WHO works to achieve this goal by promulgating international health policies and programs. Because the majority of the world's populations utilize some form of alternative medicine, WHO provides information on traditional remedies and their potential health benefits. Publications such as the *WHO Global Atlas of Traditional, Complementary and Alternative Medicine* and *Legal Status of Traditional Medicine and Complementary/Alternative Medicine: A Worldwide Review* evaluate the status of traditional and CAM modalities worldwide.

Bibliography of Books

Brent A. Bauer   *Mayo Clinic Book of Alternative Medicine.* New York: Time Inc., 2010.

R. Barker Bausell   *Snake Oil Science: The Truth About Complementary and Alternative Medicine.* New York: Oxford University Press, 2007.

Roberta E. Bivins   *Alternative Medicine?: A History.* New York: Oxford University Press, 2010.

Steven Bratman   *Complementary & Alternative Health: The Scientific Verdict on What Really Works.* London: Collins, 2007.

Robina Coker   *Complementary & Alternative Medicine: Should Christians Be Involved?* London: Christian Medical Fellowship, 2008.

Robert Davis   *The Healthy Skeptic: Cutting Through the Hype About Your Health.* Berkeley: University of California Press, 2008.

Edzard Ernst and   *Trick or Treatment?: Alternative Medicine on Trial.* London: Bantam Press, 2008.
Simon Singh

Tiffany Field   *Complementary and Alternative Therapies Research.* Washington, DC: American Psychological Association, 2009.

Ben Goldacre   *Bad Science: Quacks, Hacks, and Big Pharma Flacks.* New York: Faber and Faber, 2010.

Louise Kuo Habakus — *Vaccine Epidemic: How Corporate Greed, Biased Science, and Coercive Government Threaten Our Human Rights, Our Health, and Our Children.* New York: Skyhorse, 2011.

Bradly P. Jacobs and Katherine Gundling — *The ACP Evidence-Based Guide to Complementary & Alternative Medicine.* Philadelphia: American College of Physicians, 2009.

Lucinda E. Jesson and Stacey A. Tovino — *Complementary and Alternative Medicine and the Law.* Durham, NC: Carolina Academic Press, 2010.

Victoria Maizes and Tieraona Low Dog — *Integrative Women's Health.* Oxford and New York: Oxford University Press, 2010.

Seth Mnookin — *The Panic Virus: A True Story of Medicine, Science, and Fear.* New York: Simon & Schuster, 2011.

Michael T. Murray — *What the Drug Companies Won't Tell You and Your Doctor Doesn't Know: The Alternative Treatments That May Change Your Life—and the Prescriptions That Could Harm You.* New York: Atria Books, 2009.

National Center for Complementary and Alternative Medicine — *Exploring the Science of Complementary and Alternative Medicine: Third Strategic Plan, 2011–2015.* Bethesda, MD: US Department of Health and Human Services, National Institutes of Health, 2011.

Paul A. Offit   *Deadly Choices: How the Anti-Vaccine Movement Threatens Us All.* New York: Basic Books, 2010.

Paul A. Offit and Charlotte A. Moser   *Vaccines and Your Child: Separating Fact from Fiction.* New York: Columbia University Press, 2011.

Dónal O'Mathúna and Walter L. Larimore   *Alternative Medicine: The Christian Handbook.* Grand Rapids, MI: Zondervan, 2009.

Cynthia Ramsay   *Unnatural Regulation: Complementary and Alternative Medicine Policy in Canada.* Vancouver, BC: Fraser Institute, 2009.

Rose Shapiro   *Suckers: How Alternative Medicine Makes Fools of Us All.* London: Harville Seeker, 2008.

Richard P. Sloan   *Blind Faith: The Unholy Alliance of Religion and Medicine.* New York: St. Martin's Press, 2006.

Lois Snyder, ed.   *Complementary and Alternative Medicine: Ethics, the Patient, and the Physician.* Totowa, NJ: Humana Press, 2007.

David W. Tanton   *Antidepressants, Antipsychotics, and Stimulants: Dangerous Drugs on Trial.* Jasper, OR: Soaring Heights, 2007.

Dana Ullman   *The Homeopathic Revolution: Why Famous People and Cultural Heroes Choose Homeopathy.* Berkeley, CA: North Atlantic Books, 2007.

| Andrew J. Wakefield | *Callous Disregard: Autism and Vaccines—The Truth behind a Tragedy.* New York: Skyhorse, 2011. |

Index

A

Accidental deaths, 63, 222–223
Actuarial prediction, 123
Acupuncture, 27, 44, 152
    Asian American use, 93–94
    chi, 32–33, 49
    clinical studies, 42, 48, 49–52,
    131, 145, 148, 181, 199
    as complementary treatment,
    126, 127–128, 130, 131, 132,
    149, 151, 181–182
    cost effectiveness, 127–128,
    130, 131–132
    differences from traditional
    Chinese medicine, 145, 151–
    152
    efficacy, and "sham" acupunc-
    ture, 40–46, 47–52, 145, 165
    popularity is exaggerated, 90–
    91, 92–94, 95–97
    superficial needle stimulation,
    43, 49–50
Addictions
    pain medications, 28
    sleep aids, 25
    treatment research, 200
ADHD (attention-deficit/
    hyperactivity disorder), 137
Advertising, drugs, 164
    See also Marketing, drugs
AIDS. See HIV/AIDS
Allergy cures, 84
Alosetron, 158
Amaro, John, 47–52
American Academy of Family
    Physicians, 76

American Academy of Medical
    Preventics, 69
American Cancer Society, 16, 17,
    109
American College for Advance-
    ment in Medicine, 69, 70
American College of Cardiology,
    76
American College of Physicians,
    76
American Health Products Asso-
    ciation, 218
American Heart Association, 74,
    76
American Medical Association
    chelation therapy, 76
    failure to endorse alternative
    treatments, 98, 101
    placebo use policy, 158
American national characteristics,
    82, 84–85
American Osteopathic Association,
    76
American Society for Clinical
    Pharmacology and Therapeutics,
    76
Amri, Ramzi, 15
Amygdala (brain), 20
Anesthesia costs, 128
Angell, Marcia, 26
Angiograms, 59, 61, 62, 76
Angioplasty, 58, 59, 62, 63–64
Annenberg Foundation, 149
Anti-anxiety medications, 25
Antidepressant medications
    advertising, 164

brands and types, 169, 171
celebrity use and opinions, 106, 107
clinical trials, and results publishing, 26, 167–168, 170–171
personal experiences, 160, 169, 172–173
placebo therapy, 154, 160, 161, 162–163, 164, 167–168, 170–171, 172
side effects, 168, 169, 171, 172
Arcury, Thomas A., 140
Arm pain, 50
Armstrong, Lance, 109
Arteriograms, 59, 61, 62, 76
Arthritis
research, 165, 181
treatments, 71, 93, 114, 136, 181, 182
Aspirin, 25, 63
Association of Accredited Naturopathic Medical Colleges, 102
Asthma, 135, 137, 162, 188
Atherosclerosis. *See* Cardiovascular diseases
Atlantic (periodical), 86, 135–137, 139
Atwood, Kimball, IV, 200
Autism and vaccines, 79, 88, 105–106, 107, 108, 111
Ayurvedic medicine, 27, 149, 209

B

Bahamas, medical treatments, 16, 17
Balloon angioplasty, 54, 55, 56, 58, 59, 62, 63–64
Barnes, Patricia M., 100*t*
Bausell, R. Barker, 147

Bechler, Steve, 87
Bedell, Berkley W., 208
Bee pollen, 84
Benedetti, Fabrizio, 157
Berarducci, Arthur, 122
Berwick, Donald, 117–125
Bhanoo, Sindya N., 20
Bias
antidepressants trials results, 26, 167–168, 170–171
chelation therapy publishing, 58, 59, 64
chelation therapy studies, 61, 62
complementary therapies research (bias present), 200–203
complementary therapies research (lack of bias), 135, 136–137
homeopathy research, 34
Bioidentical hormone replacement therapy, 79
Bloodletting, 151
Bloom, Barbara, 100*t*
Blumenthal, Richard, 211–215, 216–223
Bonadonna, R., 20–21
Botanicals
calls for dietary supplement labeling requirements, 211–215
dietary supplement labeling requirements are not helpful, 216–223
medical applications studied, 180, 185–186, 198, 201, 208
Brain anatomy and chemistry
acupuncture, 42, 145, 148
meditation effects, 20, 21, 188
See also Placebo effect

Breast cancer, 105, 106, 109
Brecher, Arline, 67
Briggs, Josephine P., 200, 202, 203, 208, 209
Brown, David, 204–210
Burnham, Ted, 40–46
Bypass surgery, 54, 55, 56, 58, 59, 62, 63–64, 66
Bypassing Bypass Surgery (Cranton), 57, 67, 73

C

Caffeine, 70, 220
Calabrese, Carlo, 209–210
Cancer causes
    asbestos exposure, 16
    tobacco smoking, 31–32
Cancer screening, 105, 108, 109
Cancer treatments
    alternative medicine as supplementary, 16, 83, 101–102
    alternative medicine therapies, 85, 107, 208, 209
    alternative medicine usage rates, 16
    mesothelioma, 16–17
    surgery, 105, 106, 109
    tumors, 14–15, 16–17
Cardiovascular diseases
    mediation therapy, 21, 188
    prevention therapies, 130
    supplements, harmful interactions, 176
    tai chi therapy, 114, 130
    treatment, chelation therapy opposition, 56, 65–76
    treatment, chelation therapy support, 53–64, 70–71

CARE (clinical applications of research evidence) construct, 135, 138–139
Carroll, Aaron, 107, 111
Carter, J.P., 71, 75
Carter, Rosalynn, 108
Celebrities, influence, 79–80, 88, 105–111
Celebrity doctors, 15–16, 83, 85, 86, 88, 110, 111, 203
Center for Health Value Innovation, 129
Centers for Disease Control and Prevention (CDC)
    chelation therapy, 76
    National Health Interview Survey (NHIS), 92, 93, 99–100, 100*t*, 102, 181
Centers for Medicare and Medicaid Services, 117–118
Chao, Samantha M., 117–125
Chaucer, Geoffrey, 155
Chelation therapy
    costs, 70
    dangerous and ineffective for most conditions, 65–76
    history, 68–69
    lack of laws against, 56–57
    process described, 60, 69–70
    safe and effective for many conditions, 53–64
Chi (acupuncture), 32–33, 49
Chinese Canadians and Americans, 93–94
Chinese medicine, 94–95, 145, 149, 151–152
Chiropractic medicine
    as complementary treatment, 126, 127, 128–129, 130

cost effectiveness, 128–129
user totals, 92, 130
Cho, Zang-Hee, 148–149
Chopra, Deepak, 85, 88
Choudry, N., 129
Chromium supplementation, 136–137, 198
Chronic care model, 123
Chronic diseases, 85, 98–99, 101
avoidance through healthy habits, 182
lifestyle treatments/management, 103
Cigna, 127–128
Claim management, 128
Clarke, C.N., 68
Clarke, N.E., 68
Clement, John, 17
Clinical studies and trials
acupuncture, 42, 48, 49–52, 131, 145, 148, 181, 199
antidepressants, 26, 167–168, 170–171
chelation therapy, 55, 57–58, 59, 61–62, 64, 65–66, 68–69, 71–73, 74–75, 76
complementary medicine and profits, 144–145, 147
complementary medicine approach, 131–133, 134–135, 186–189, 205
duration, pharmaceutical industry, 25, 26, 87
fraud, 26
grant types, 194–197, 198–199
homeopathy, 29–30, 33–34, 35–36, 38–39, 165, 199–200
medications vs. placebos, 153, 154, 155–157, 158
meditation, 20–21, 131

mind-body medicine, 114–115, 187–188
more needed for alternative medicine, 101, 131–133, 135–136, 180, 183, 185
pro-conventional medicine bias, 23–24, 24–25, 26, 29
Clum, Gerard, 129, 130, 132–133
Colitis, 51
Colorectal cancer screening, 108
Complementary medical treatment approach
can lower costs, 126–133
dangers of discounting wholly, 137–138
helps patients and is scientifically sound, 134–143
is scientifically unsound and profit-focused, 144–152
See also Integrative medicine
Conditioning, psychological, 157–158, 163–164, 172
Constitution of the United States, 14
Consumer-driven service models, 121–123
Conventional medicine
frustration with, 98–104, 141
reliance on medications, 23–24
"scientism," 28, 29, 30, 31, 136, 139–140, 142–143
used following alternative medicine, 15, 103–104
Cooper, David, 80
Costs of health care
complementary treatments can lower costs, 126–133, 184
prescription drugs, 28, 57
traditional, 100

Council for Responsible Nutrition, 176–177
Couric, Katie, 108, 109
Covi, Uno, 160
Cox, Lauren, 98–104
Cranton, Elmer M., 53–64, 67, 69, 73
Cruise, Tom, 107
Cures, caveats, 16, 28

D

Dartmouth Institute for Health Policy Research, 121
de Goya, Francisco, 146
Debas, Haile T., 147
Depression
    celebrities addressing, 106, 107
    herbal remedies, 87–88
    mind-body therapies, 115, 130, 131
    placebo antidepressants, 154, 160, 161, 162–163, 164, 167–168, 170–171, 172
Diabetes
    alternative medicine inappropriate, 101
    alternative medicine sought, 83
    tai chi therapy, 114
Diehm, Curt, 62, 72
Diet pills, 176, 177
Diet-related therapies, 130
    cancer treatment, 14
    preventive care, 182, 201
Dietary Supplement Health and Education Act (1994), 84, 214
Dietary Supplement Labeling Act (2011)
    con- stance, 216–223
    pro- stance, 211–215

Dietary supplements
    expanding labeling requirements should be expanded, 211–215
    expanding labeling requirements should not be expanded, 216–223
    quackery debate, 55
    regulation, 82, 83, 84, 87, 176–177, 211–215, 216–223
    research, 185–186, 198
    safety issues, 102, 176–177, 212–213, 215, 217, 219, 222–223
    usage, 99, 100*t*, 102, 127
Dilution, in homeopathy, 36, 37, 199
The Dinner Game (film), 152
Direct-to-consumer advertising, 164
Diverticulitis, 51
Doctor-patient relationships
    artistic portrayals, 145–146
    doctors can use placebo treatments, 153–166
    personal attention, positive effects, 154, 158, 159, 163, 164–165, 170
    placebo treatment can have harmful or beneficial effects, 167–173
    time spent, visits, 103, 165–166
    See also Health care, US; Patient-centered care
Dosages
    chelation therapy, 60
    homeopathy vs. conventional medicine, 31, 32
    low, as placebo treatment, 160, 161

Double-blind trials
    absent, traditional medical
        procedures, 55–56
    chelation therapy, 55–56, 66,
        71, 72, 75, 76
    costs, 57
    impossible, acupuncture, 52
    pharmaceuticals, 24, 29, 30,
        57, 171
Drug companies. *See* Pharmaceuti-
    cal industry
Drug safety. *See* Safety, drugs
Durbin, Dick, 211–215, 216–223

E

Echinacea, 102, 208
Efficacy
    acupuncture, true vs. sham,
        40–46, 47–52, 165
    alternative therapies, 101, 130,
        133–139, 194
    botanical dietary supplements,
        185–186
    decreased efficacy, and drug
        replacement, 26–27
    homeopathy, 33
    pharmaceutical oversight, 87
    placebos, 25, 153, 154, 156–
        158, 163–164
    terminology challenges, 24–25,
        28
*The Emperor's New Drugs: Explod-
    ing the Antidepressant Myth*
    (Kirsch), 160, 162, 170–171, 172
Employee absenteeism, reducing,
    126–127, 128, 129
Enblom, Anna, 44, 45
Energy drinks, 212–213, 217–218,
    218–220
Ephedra, 87
Ernst, Edzard, 35–39

Ethical placebo use, 153–154, 157–
    158, 160, 161–166
Ethylenediaminetetraacetic acid
    (EDTA), 68
    chelation therapy, 53, 58, 60,
        62–63, 66, 68
    criticisms, 55, 61, 63, 66
    patent protection expiration,
        56, 57
Every Child By Two
    (immunization campaign), 108
Evidence-based medicine
    discounting complementary
        therapies, 17, 101, 137–138,
        140–141, 142, 191–193
    evidence focus as limitation of
        medicine, 27, 29, 137–138
    providing, for complementary
        therapies, and NCCAM
        goals, 181, 183, 185–186,
        187, 188–189
    See also Science-based medi-
        cine
Exercise
    chelation therapy/outcome
        measurement, 62, 70, 71, 72
    included as complementary
        and alternative medicine, 92,
        99, 102, 130, 182
    tai chi, 114–115, 130, 182
    yoga, 135, 137, 182
    See also Mind-body medicine
Extramural research
    basic, 183, 185–186
    clinical, 186–189

F

Family members, patients', 121,
    124, 125
FDA. *See* Food and Drug Adminis-
    tration (FDA)

Federal Trade Commission (FTC), 56, 76

Fibromyalgia, 93, 115, 137, 182, 208–209

Fineberg, Harvey, 118–119

Fluidity of evidence, 29, 135–136, 138–139

Food, marketed as dietary supplements, 212–213, 214, 217–218, 218–220

Food and Drug Administration (FDA)

  Adverse Events Reporting System, 222

  antidepressant studies withheld, 171

  chelation therapy, 56–57, 64, 74, 76

  dietary supplements regulation, 82, 84, 88, 176–177, 212–215, 217, 219, 220–223

  immuno augmentative therapy ban, 17

  pharmaceutical approval role, 25, 56, 87, 156, 167, 171

  political relations, 84, 214, 217, 220–222

  sibutramine notification, 176

Food Safety Modernization Act (2011), 217, 220–222

Ford, Betty, 105, 106, 109

Ford Motor Company, 127, 130–132

Fox, Michael J., 106

Freedom of Information Act (1966), 171

Friedson, Eliot, 122

Functional magnetic resonance imaging (fMRI), 148

Fundraising, celebrity, 109

Funeral customs, 155

G

Gastrointestinal distress, 51

Gay, John, 219

Genomics, 123

Goldacre, Ben, 165

Gordon, Garry, 67

Gorski, David, 86, 147, 191–203

Grant types, 194–197, 198–199

Green, Saul

  addressed by chelation therapy supporter, 53–54, 55, 56, 57, 59, 61, 62, 63–64

  chelation therapy is dangerous and ineffective, 65–76

Grzywacz, Joseph G., 140

H

Hahnemann, Samuel, 34, 37

Harkin, Tom, 84, 87, 184, 201, 206, 207–208

Hatch, Orrin, 84, 87, 222

Headaches

  acupuncture treatments, 48

  homeopathic treatments, 30

Healing

  integrative medicine focus, 121, 122–123, 124, 125, 138, 141

  medication use, vs. natural, 26–28, 29

  placebo use and success, 153–154, 156, 157–158, 160, 164

Health, defined, 122–123

Health care, US

  cost savings methods, 118, 126–133

costs, annual, 100
fragmented nature, 119, 120
frustration with traditional
    medicine, 98–104, 141
National Center for Comple-
    mentary and Alternative
    Medicine offerings, 179–183
need for improvements, and
    integrative medicine, 117–
    125, 184
need for improvements, and
    naturopathic medicine, 103
quality issues and initiatives,
    120
See also Health insurance
Health insurance
    benefits, complementary and
        alternative therapies, 127–
        128, 140
    changes, predictive health
        care, 123
    complementary and alterna-
        tive therapies not yet cov-
        ered, 132
    naturopathic care without,
        103
Heavy metal removal, chelation
    therapy, 60, 68, 70, 71
Herbal remedies. *See* Botanicals
Herper, Matthew, 161
Hesse, Bradford, 107, 109
Hippocampus (brain), 20
History, 30–31, 34
HIV/AIDS
    massage, 137
    patient drug interactions,
        87–88
    screening, 108
Homeopathic medicine
    clinical studies, 29–30, 33–34,
        35–36, 38–39, 165, 199–200

conventional medicine's nega-
    tive characterizations, 23,
    31–34
history, 32, 37
is effective, 23–34
is ineffective, 35–39, 137
principles, 37
Homeopathy (journal), 33
Hopf, R., 72–73
Hormone replacement therapy, 79
Hospitals, 88–89
Hui, Ka-Kit, 149
Human resources, 125
Hyman, Mark, 88
Hyper- and hypothyroidism, 79

I

The Imaginary Invalid (Molière),
    145–146
Immune system
    health, mediation therapy, 21,
        188
    immuno augmentative
        therapy (IAT), 16, 17
Individualized medicine. *See*
    Patient-centered care
Industry profits, 83, 88, 99, 100,
    100*t*, 181
Infant mortality rates, 28
Informed placebo use, 153–154,
    157–158, 160, 161–166
Innovation, American, 84–85
Institute for Healthcare Improve-
    ment, 117, 118, 121, 122
Institute of Medicine, 117, 118,
    120, 123
Insulin resistance, 136–137
Insurance. *See* Health insurance
Integrative medicine
    advantages, 117–125, 135

appropriate treatments, 15–16, 103–104

attacks on, 86, 134–136, 139–140, 142–143, 147, 149, 151–152, 207

core principles, 118, 121, 123–125, 138, 139, 184

tai chi research and application, 114–115

See also Complementary medical treatment approach

Internet, information distribution

blogging about NCCAM, 200, 205, 207–208

reliability of information, 106, 111

Wikipedia, 168–169

Intramural research, 189–190

Irritable bowel syndrome (IBS), 157–158, 161–162, 165, 166

Isaacson, Walter, 14–15

Israelson, Loren, 219, 220, 222

J

Japanese acupuncture, 50, 51

Jobs, Steve, 14–15

Johnson, Magic, 108

Jones, Val, 147

Journal of Clinical Epidemiology, 33

K

Kaptchuk, Ted, 157–158, 161, 165

Karolinska Institute, 43, 148

Katz, David, 134–143

Kavoussi, Ben, 144–152

Kirsch, Irving, 154, 157–158, 160–166, 170–171, 172

Kitchell, J. Roderick, 59, 69

Kosova, Weston, 80

Koster, Kathleen, 126–133

Kupka, Thomas, 101–102

L

Labeling. *See* Dietary Supplement Labeling Act (2011)

Lancing, 151

Lang, Wei, 140

Langreth, Robert, 161

Law of similars (homeopathy), 37

Lead poisoning, 67

Life expectancy rates, 28

Lifestyle changes, 103, 182, 188

Loomis, Marnie, 102, 103

Lyme disease, 208

M

Mammograms, 105, 109

Maori health care (New Zealand), 124

Marijuana, 169

Marketing, drugs, 28, 56, 58, 164

Massage

AIDS care, 137

as complementary treatment, 127, 181–182

osteoarthritis treatment, 136

Mastectomies, 105, 106, 109

Mayo Clinic, 122, 123

McCarthy, Jenny, 79, 88, 105–106, 107, 108, 111

McGinnis, J. Michael, 117–125

McGuffin, Michael, 218, 220, 221–222

McKenzie, Brennen, 90–97

"Meaning response," 172

"Medical chauvinism," 29

Medical freedom, 14

Medical publishing
 acupuncture reports, 41–43, 48, 49–51, 148–149
 bias issues, 26, 31, 58, 59, 64, 135, 136–137, 167–168
 complaints, science journalism, 41–43, 46, 135–136, 142
 evidence of failed treatments, 135, 136–137
 Internet, legitimacy concerns, 106, 111, 168
 placebo use reports, 156, 165
 retractions, 148–149
 sham studies, 58
Medical Society of the City and County of New York, 34
Meditation
 effectiveness and positive outcomes, 20–21, 127, 131, 182, 188
 usage studies, 127, 130–131, 180, 187–188
Melatonin products, 214, 217, 219
Meltzer, Lawrence E., 59, 68
Menopausal symptoms and treatments, 186, 188
Mercury poisoning, 67
Mesothelioma, 16–17
MetaboLife, 87
Migraine headaches
 acupuncture treatments, 48
 homeopathic treatments, 30
Milstein, A., 129
Minchin, Tim, 89
Mind-body medicine
 as complementary therapy, 126, 128, 130, 182, 187
 research, 182, 187, 199, 209
 tai chi and qigong, 114–115, 130

Mindfulness mediation, 21, 187–188, 209
Mister, Steve, 176–177
Mittman, Paul, 103
Moerman, Dan, 159, 163
Moffet, Howard H., 42
Molière, 145–146
Morphine, 36
Mosher, R.E., 68
Myers, Martin, 109
Myers, P.Z., 165

N

Nahin, Richard, 99–100, 100t
National Cancer Institute, 107, 110–111, 207
National Center for Complementary and Alternative Medicine (NCCAM)
 budget, 185, 187, 189, 190, 193, 200, 204–205, 206, 207
 consumer education, 88
 establishment and purpose, 84, 101, 179–180, 184, 192, 193–194, 200, 205–206
 funding from FDA, 82
 should be funded, 179–190
 should not be funded, 191–203, 206
 training programs, 188–189, 193–194, 197
 value is unclear, 204–210
National College of Natural Medicine, 102, 209–210
National Health Interview Survey (NHIS), 92, 93, 99–100, 100t, 102, 181
National Institutes of Health (NIH)

budget, 84, 193, 200, 204–205, 206, 207
chelation therapy, 76
grant types, 194–197, 198–199
National Center for Complementary and Alternative Medicine research projects, 185–190, 192, 194–197, 202–203
National Health Interview Survey (NHIS), 92, 93, 99–100, 100*t*, 102, 181
Office of Alternative Medicine, 184
reports, alternative medicine, 99
structure, 206
See also National Center for Complementary and Alternative Medicine (NCCAM)
National Network for Immunization Information, 109
National Research Council, 76
"Natural" products
dietary supplements, safety issues, 102, 176, 219
dietary supplements, usage, 100*t*, 127
research, 185–186, 198, 201, 208
See also Botanicals; Dietary supplements
Naturopathic medicine
growing use, 98–99
methodology, 24, 27, 102–104
practitioner education, 102, 209–210
See also Acupuncture; Homeopathic medicine
Nausea reduction treatments, 40–41, 41–42, 43–44
Nazi Germany, 39

NCCAM. *See* National Center for Complementary and Alternative Medicine (NCCAM)
Neuroplasticity, 20, 188
New England Journal of Medicine, 26
New Zealand, 124
Newman, David, 172
Nguyen, Ha T., 140
"Nocebo" effect, 168, 171–172
Northrup, Christiane, 80, 88
Novella, Steve, 83, 207
Nutrition information labeling, 219, 220
Nutritional therapies, 128, 130, 137
See also Dietary supplements

O

Obama, Barack
appointments, 117–118
science policy, 206
Offit, Paul, 109, 111
Olszewer, E., 71, 75
Osher Center for Integrative Medicine, 147–148
Osteoarthritis, 136, 181, 182
Out-of-pocket costs, alternative therapies, 99, 100, 100*t*, 102, 181
Over-the-counter medications, 63
Oz, Mehmet, 83, 85, 88, 110, 111

P

Pain medications
vs. homeopathy, 36
placebos, 156, 161, 162
short-term relief, 28
work safety regulations, 131–132

Pain treatments, 181–182
  acupuncture, 50, 92, 93, 96, 127, 130, 148, 181, 209
  chiropractic care, 128–129
  meditation, 188
  placebos, 156, 161, 162
  tai chi, 115, 130, 209
Panic attacks, 25
Parikh, Rahul, 82–89, 110
Paris, A., 36, 38
Park, Lee, 160
Parkinson's disease, 71, 106, 114, 156, 162
Patient-centered care
  homeopathy, 32
  integrative medicine does not provide, 146–149
  integrative medicine provides, 118, 120–124, 138, 139–141
  naturopathy, 103–104
  traditional health care, care vs. control, 120–121, 139, 141
Patient interviews
  doctor visits, 166
  homeopathic medicine, 32
  National Health Interview Survey, 92, 93, 99–100, 100t, 102, 181
Pauling, Linus, 69
Pavlov, Ivan, 157–158, 163
Peet, Amanda, 111
Pelletier, Kenneth R., 128, 130
Personal attention, from doctors, 154, 158, 159, 163, 164–165, 170
Personalized medicine. See Patient-centered care
Pharmaceutical industry
  chelation therapy interests, 54, 55, 58, 62
  criticisms of drug trials and safety policies, 23–24, 25–27
  drug costs, 28, 57
  lauding of drug trials and safety policies, 87
  marketing, 28, 56, 58, 164
  placebo success outcomes, 156, 158, 160
  placebo vs. drug efficacy, 153, 154, 155–157, 158
  prescription rates/ polypharmacy, 27
  profit focus and goals, 23–24
  profit statistics, 29, 58
  See also Dietary supplements
Pharmaceutical-tainted dietary supplements, 176–177
Phillips, Ruth, 16–17
Physical therapy, 127, 129, 131
Physician-patient relationships. See Doctor-patient relationships
Phytoestrogens, 186
Picker Institute, 121–122
Pisani, Amy, 108, 111
Placebo-controlled trials, 153, 154, 155–157
  absent, traditional medical procedures, 55–56
  chelation therapy, 55–56, 72–73, 75, 76
  pharmaceuticals, 24, 29–30, 38, 171
Placebo effect
  acupuncture, 40, 43, 45, 47, 49, 96, 154, 165
  chelation therapy, 57, 75
  defined and described, 45, 154, 155, 156, 162, 163–164, 168–169, 209–210

doctor attention and empathy, 154, 158, 159, 163, 164–165, 170

effectiveness rates, 25, 153, 154, 156–158, 210

homeopathy, 36, 37, 38–39, 154, 165

treatment enhancement, 160, 161

withdrawal and harmful symptoms, 168, 171–172

See also Placebo treatments

"Placebo," terminology, 154–155, 159

Placebo treatments

can have harmful or beneficial effects, 167–173

doctors can and should use, ethically, 153–166

See also Placebo effect

Politics and culture influence, alternative medicine, 79–80, 82–89, 94, 105–111

Polypharmacy, 27

Popularity of alternative medicine

celebrity influence, 79–80, 88, 105–111

complementary therapies and cost savings, 126–127, 130

exaggerated, 90–97

naturopathy, 103–104

politics and culture influence, 82–89, 94

reflects frustration with traditional medicine, 84, 98–104

total users, 181

See also National Health Interview Survey (NHIS)

Potentation, in homeopathy, 36, 37, 199

Predictive health care systems, 123

Preventive medicine

disease screening, 105, 108–109

healthy habits value in CAM, 86, 182, 201

mind-body, 114

Proceedings of the National Academy of Sciences (periodical), 148–149

"Proving" (homeopathy), 37

Pseudoscience, 86, 107, 201, 203, 205, 206

Psychiatry, 107

Publishing, history, 31

Publishing, medical. *See* Medical publishing

Q

Qigong, 114–115, 200

"Quackery"

chelation therapy debate, 53–64, 65–76

complementary therapies accusations, 86, 134–136, 139–140, 142–143, 147, 164–165

defining, 29, 31

"sham" acupuncture, 40–46

See also Pseudoscience

Quality of care

industry-defined, 122, 123

patient-defined, 122

quality initiatives, 120

Quan, H., 93–94

R

Radiation therapy, 16, 40, 43–44

Raz, Amir, 160

Reagan, Nancy, 109

Reiki, 94, 201, 208–209

Research, complementary and alternative medicine
  criticisms, 142, 144–145, 147–149, 151–152, 191–192, 193, 207
  NCCAM programs, 180, 181–183, 185–190, 191–192, 193, 197–203, 207
  needs for, 101, 131–133, 135–136, 180, 183, 185
  placebo therapy, 154, 157–158, 159–166
  as unbiased and relevant, 134–135, 136–137
  See also Clinical studies and trials
Rheumatoid arthritis, 165
Richards, Byron J., 221
Rotavirus, 111
Rowland, Julia, 110
Runestad, Todd, 216–223
Rush, Benjamin, 14
Ruth L. Kirschstein National Research Service Award, 189

S

Safety, drugs
  pharmaceutical-tainted dietary supplements, 176–177
  replacement, unsafe products, 26–27
  side effects, 25, 27, 28
Salzburg, Steven, 206
Sampson, Wally, 192–193, 200
Schultz, Andrea M., 117–125
Schultz, Hank, 216–223
Schwarzenegger, Arnold, 151
Science-based medicine, 86
  alternative health care, 184, 208

  alternative medicine is not, 192–193, 202, 207
  supporting publications and sites, 144
  See also "Scientism"
Scientific advances, American history, 84–85
Scientific method, 24, 142–143, 193, 208
Scientific publishing. See Medical publishing
"Scientism," 28, 29, 30, 31, 136, 139–140, 142–143
Self-regulation, supplement industry, 84, 177
Serotonin, 162–163
"Sham" acupuncture, 40–46, 47–52, 145, 165
Sherry, Wendy, 127–128
Shields, Brooke, 106, 107
Shomon, Mary, 80
Sibutramine, 176
Silberman, Steve, 153–166
Singer, Natasha, 176, 177
Skepticism, 33, 85, 158
Sleep-aid drugs, 25
Sleep studies, 199
Smoking, 31–32, 188
Sobel, Eliezer, 167–173
The Social Transformation of American Medicine (Starr), 85
Somers, Suzanne, 79, 88, 107, 111
Spinal manipulation, 181–182
St. John's wort, 87–88
StarCaps (supplement), 177
Starr, Paul, 85
Straus, Stephen, 200, 202
Stress reduction
  mediation therapy, 20–21, 187–188

mind-body interventions, 114, 130, 182
Stringer, Korey, 87
Stussman, Barbara J., 100*t*
Surgery
    avoidance, chelation therapy, 54, 57, 58–59, 60, 63–64, 66, 67, 73
    cancer, 105, 106, 109
    deaths, 63
    decisions against, 14–15
    recovery therapies, 130
    trials, 29
    unproven nature, 55
Surveys. *See* National Health Interview Survey (NHIS)
Susan Samueli Center for Integrative Medicine, 147, 149
Symptom management
    complementary/alternative medicine, 181–182, 183, 187
    symptom-treating nature of drugs, 23, 25
Szabo, Liz, 105–111

T

Tai chi, 114–115, 130, 182, 187, 209
Taiwan, 94–95
Talamonti, Walter J., 131, 132
Tate, Ryan, 15
Taylor, Elizabeth, 106
Technology advances
    American science history, 84–85
    enabling individualized medicine, 123
Therapeutic touch, 209
Thyroid disease, 79–80

Traditional Chinese medicine (TCM), 94–95, 145, 149, 151–152
Training programs, NCCAM, 188–189, 193–194, 197
Translational research, 183, 185, 190
Traumatic injuries, treatment, 15–16
Trowbridge, John Parks, 67

U

Ullman, Dana, 23–34, 38
United States Constitution, 14
United States' health ranking, 28
University of California, 88, 128, 145, 147–149, 151
US Customs Service, 176
US Food and Drug Administration (FDA). *See* Food and Drug Administration (FDA)

V

Vaccines, childhood, 79, 88, 105–106, 107, 108, 109, 111
Varmus, Harold, 206
Venipuncture, 151–152
"Vital force" (homeopathy), 32–33
Vitamins
    chelation therapy, 60, 70
    supplements, 55, 214–215, 220
    See also Dietary supplements

W

Wager, Tor, 157
Wagner, Edward, 123
Walker, Morton, 67
Walkup, Michael, 140

Wang Guoqiang, 149, 151

Weight loss supplements, 176, 177

Weil, Andrew, 15–16, 86, 203

Wikipedia, 168–169

Winfrey, Oprah, 79–80

Wingert, Patricia, 80

Wong, Jason, 170

Workplace absences, reduction methods, 126–127, 128, 129

World Health Organization (WHO), 142

X

Xanax, 25

Y

Yoga
  benefits, 182, 187
  ineffective asthma treatment, 135, 137

Z

Zinc, 68, 71, 73–74

ZOL Consultants, 55